I could hear voices around me. I sensed their anxiety but I felt too drowsy to make out what they were saying. It seemed like forever but it was probably only five minutes before I felt the pressure of a tube being forced down my throat. It was very frightening. I was only thirteen and this was my first overdose. As the doctors worked on my body I began to see things more clearly, though the voices still sounded distant. I knew then that I wasn't going to die. I never really wanted to die; I simply did not want to live...

ROXANNE

There are only two forces in this world; the swordand the spirit, and in the long run the sword will always be conquered by the spirit.

Napoleon Bonaparte

ROXANNE

MY EXTRAORDINARY LIFE

ROXANNE HOLMES

Copyright © 2014 Roxanne Holmes

First published in Australia and New Zealand in 1996
jointly by Millenium Books and Random House Australia

Published by Vivid Publishing
A division of Fontaine Publishing Group
P.O. Box 948 Fremantle
Western Australia 6959
www.vividpublishing.com.au

National Library of Australia cataloguing-in-publication data:
Author: Holmes, Roxanne, author.
Title: Roxanne : my extraordinary life / Roxanne Holmes.
Edition: 2nd revised edition.
ISBN: 9781925086751 (paperback)
Subjects: Holmes, Roxanne.
           Adult child abuse victims--Australia--Biography.
           Drug addicts--Australia--Biography.
Dewey Number: 362.76092

acknowledgments

This book is dedicated to:

"Arty and Paul" - two beautiful souls who have taught me love and courage. I also want to thank the following :

Arizona for the joy she brings into my life. James, Louise, Shyamma, Bayleigh, Jake, April. Poppy , Pastor Roy and Gae Barrett and members of peninsula Vineyard church, Em, lee, Lorraine and family.

Maxelle, Dorothy, Jenny, Musa and Jasmine, Temgaze "Adira-Belle", Benzelewe my beloved Godson. Talakai, Georgia H, Courtney, Anne, Staff at Relationships Australia. Lifeline Australia, Deborah L,

Jack, Cassie and Eve, Paul Barry and family, Fiona, Andrea and all those whom have walked with me throughout my journey and have encouraged me to continue writing.

I would like to personally thank Mr Jason Swiney of Fontaine Publishing Group for believing in my journey. Oprah Winfrey for her empowerment of women and children everywhere. Lastly I want to acknowledge the Daniel Morcombe Foundation for highlighting and educating the importance of child safety.

Roxanne

introduction

In 1996 "Roxanne: My Extraordinary Life" was first published. For me the success was always measured by the hands and lives my story has touched. My deepest desire was for my journey to show no matter where you come from, or what struggles you may face, with hope you can overcome your hardships. After the initial release of my story I received hundreds of letters from teenagers, parents, police and professionals from around the world, all sharing their own stories. I was really moved by the overwhelming response and interest in my journey. I had shared many of my personal experiences but still was struggling with severe dissociative disorder and anxiety which I had suppressed; memories of horrific early childhood abuse. Although I had little insight, I now have hindsight and have been able to finally answer my own questions.

In my quest to find myself, in 1999, I met Arty, an ordinary man who taught me extraordinary things. He was my inspiration to change. Arty gave me the gift of love and life, a life through my faith which has kept me alive. I have established my own ministry Roxanne Holmes Ministries in which I encourage teens and empower young women who have experienced trauma to find themselves. In the past few years I have been asked "what happened next". I decided after setting up my ministry that it was time to complete my journey, Part Two. I have always chosen to heal my life and am finally now receiving the help and love that I always strived so hard to find. Due to the high demand for my book, we decided to republish it. My follow-up book "Meet me at the Cross"is due to be released later in 2014. Although I have endured years of suffering, I am finally breaking the chains which have held me down for so long .

Life is not about avoiding the storms but rather learning to dance in the rain.

Roxanne

contents

❧

england

⚜

Iremember the pain and blackness of growing up as a rejected and abused child. Relationships, even the bad ones, develop in subtle ways. I don't recall exactly when the abuse first started; it seems as though it was always there. In 1970 I was four years old. My parents named me Elizabeth Lee. They both rejected me from a very early age: there were no cuddles, no kisses—no affection. I had two sisters: Sofia was the eldest and Larissa was a year younger than me. Jacob, our father, was in the Army, and we children were always told that he also worked for British Intelligence—the secret service. My parents had recently divorced, and my father had been posted to Germany, where he now lived with his new wife. I lived with my mother and sisters in the ancient city of Canterbury, in a three-bedroomed suburban house. Our house held many secrets.

Later on, Madeleine, my mother, used to tell me stories about how my father had abused her. She said he had pushed her downstairs when she was pregnant with my younger sister, and had then beaten her so badly that she haemorrhaged and was rushed to hospital by ambulance. Somehow she seemed to transfer all the blame for this abuse to me. Sometimes she would set about punishing me in a very systematic way. For hours I would be made to stand facing the wall. My mother called this "sending me to Coventry". Every day I would be emotionally abused. Sometimes she would lock me inside a dark cupboard. I remember how I would cry out to her and to my sisters, but no one answered me. The only sound I could hear was the frantic beating of my heart. I was terrified. I prayed to God to make my dad come and get me, but this never happened. While I was living in fear and misery, Dad was acting the part of the dutiful husband in Germany. At four and a half years old I felt dead inside.

At other times my mother would lash out indiscriminately and beat all three of us. She told Larissa and Sofia not to talk to me—if they did, she said she would beat them black-and-blue. Immediately after my father left, while the divorce was pending, the beatings got worse. Mum would drag me into the living room and begin to punch me. She told me that if I moved I would get more. There was nothing I could do about it, I just had to lie there and take the savage attack. I hated the way my mother treated me and I hated my sisters. Most of all I hated myself.

Yet in some strange way, even at that early age, I under-stood that my mother did not enjoy hurting me. With hindsight, I realise that she herself was a victim of rejection and domestic violence. My father's abuse and his eventual rejection of her caused enormous stress. I was the only one of her daughters who resembled my father, and having a child who was the spitting image of her husband didn't exactly help matters.

One day, together with three of the neighbouring children—we were all aged about four—I wandered off to the railway tracks. They were electrified, but being so little, we had no idea of the potential danger. Luckily we were spotted by a policeman, who detained us and then got in touch with our parents. My mother arrived to collect me. She didn't say a word until we got home, and then I was beaten. She said I had put everyone to a great deal of trouble—the policeman had told her that all the trains had been halted between Canterbury and London. But she said nothing about any fears she might have had for my safety. I craved love. All those other children

I knew had loving and caring parents, but I had no idea what real affection was.

Another time, my mother took me into the city and told me not to go near the busy traffic on the road. She said I might be run over and killed. My response was to run right in front of a car. I wanted to go to Heaven. I thought that if I died she would not be so unhappy herself. I knew I made her miserable. I knew it was my own fault she was so violent. My mother was incapable of expressing her emotions in any other way. There was only one way she could get close to me, and it hurt so much. I just accepted everything that happened. The more she hurt me, the more I needed her. When we went shopping she would make me steal chocolate bars. I really wanted to please her and would walk out of the shops with my loot. One day I was caught by a check-out girl. My mother pretended she was horrified, and told me off in front of everyone. I was very confused, and of course when we got home she beat me because I'd been caught.

Without my father, my mother found it difficult to make ends meet, so she took a job in a local restaurant. My sisters and I would be left alone at home. About this time, Mum met a man called Allen, who worked at the local supermarket. He used to visit us, bringing lollies and toys, and one day he invited Larissa and me to his house while Mum was working. Allen was weird, and so was his house. He wasn't married and lived alone in this dark, smelly cottage. We thought he was real creepy. Once inside his place he led us into an attic room and said that he wanted to play a game with us. As we walked upstairs he said it would be lots of fun, and promised us more lollies. Then he told us to take off our clothes—he had a funny look on his face. After I had undressed he unzipped his pants and sexually assaulted me. He did the same to Larissa, who was really only a baby still. I began to cry. I wanted to go home. That day my innocence was taken from me.

Allen had violated me in a way that damaged my mind as well as my body and his assault instilled in me a very deep fear. I knew that what he'd done to us was not right. Later, when my mother arrived to pick us up, Allen told her we were crying because we'd been missing her. An outright lie. Yet I was scared to tell my mother the truth, because I was afraid of her reaction. As for Larissa, she hadn't even learned to talk properly yet.

After that incident with Allen I began to wet my bed. When this happened my mother would yell and scream and hit me. She told me I was evil, just like my father. (I couldn't help reminding her of him every time she looked at me.)

A few years later, I discovered that as well as suffering domestic violence, my mother had been abused as a child. She was abandoned as a baby and knew what it was like to feel rejected even before my father left her. I asked myself how she could pass on the same experiences to her own children. But it wasn't just my mother, it was my father as well. I felt enormous rejection from my father, and although I remembered that he and Mum both used to abuse me, I still needed him. I needed his love.

Then it happened. I saw my father again. After a lot of argument between my parents, my mother agreed that I could go to Germany. Dad came to Canterbury to collect me, and I flew off with him to Dusseldorf, where he was stationed. Isabel, my stepmother, doted on me and brought me pretty dresses and dolls. Yet all the time I was there, in spite of all the new things I was given, the deep-seated fear caused by Allen's sexual assault hung over me like a dark shadow.

My father decided to give a party for my fifth birthday. My very first party. Lots of little German children came along to celebrate my existence. I wondered why. Once the party was over, the joy soon evaporated. After the last guest had gone, my father suddenly reverted to his former behaviour and threw me against a concrete wall. I ended up in hospital with a cracked skull. The doctors were told I'd had a bad fall. No one bothered to ask a crying five-year-old what had really happened. Child abuse was not commonly talked about twenty years ago. Another two months went by, and then my father made plans to ship me back to England, to my mother. He told me the Secret Service was posting him to a mysterious destination and I would not be allowed to go with him.

So Dad and I flew back to England. As soon as we arrived on the doorstep of our house in Canterbury, I remembered everything that had happened there and fear came flooding back. "Please don't leave me, Dad!" I begged, while my mother screamed out: "I don't want her!" Larissa, who was sitting on the floor, began to cry loudly. "Can't you shut that thing up?" my father shouted, then kicked her across the room with his Army boots. As my parents argued and screamed at each other, I began to cry too. I really wanted to stay with my father. When Dad left, he told me he would come back to get me soon. He promised he would not leave me with my mother forever. After that, I used to wait for him, sitting on the doorstep, every day, but he never came back. I wish he hadn't lied to me.

Most of my childhood was spent in cycles of periodic abuse, and I ended up thinking this was a normal way of life. By this time my older sister, Sofia, was a boarding pupil at the Convent of the Nativity at Sittingbourne, a town in Kent between Canterbury and London. Now I was sent off to join her there. When the holidays came around, my mother called the school to let them know she would be unable to look after me; she asked if I could stay there instead of coming home. This convinced me once and for all that my mother loathed me. I think the truth was that the very sight of me drove her mad. I ended up spending the rest of that summer with the nuns, but I didn't mind. At least they cared for me properly.

My family was not Catholic, but as I grew up I found that

I liked the Catholic faith—when it suited me. Children came to the Convent of the Nativity from all over the world. It was a red-brick building dating from the early 1900s, surrounded by extensive grounds with tall trees. We slept in draughty, high-roofed dormitories. Sister Philomena was the head sister in charge of the school. Sofia and I were sent there, of course, because my mother did not want us at home.

perth

❧

In 1974 my mother made a momentous decision. We would emigrate to Australia. In December the following year we arrived in Perth. I was now eight years old. Once again I was separated from my mother; as part of the Migrant Settlers Scheme, my mother had arranged for my younger sister Larissa and me to be placed in Fairbridge Farm School, originally an orphanage for British children sent to Australia after World War II.

At Fairbridge we were placed in one of the open cottages in Pinjarra. But it wasn't like living in a real home. The Farm School was just another institution for parents to offload their unwanted kids. I used to cry myself to sleep and dream about having a mum and dad who loved and wanted me. Life at Fairbridge could be cruel. I remember how we were forced to eat up all the food on our plates every night. However much we might dislike something that had been served up to us, we had to finish every scrap. One evening I spat out some beetroot, and I was made to go on eating it until I vomited. Then I had to swallow the vomit surrounding the remaining beetroot. I threw most of it under the table.

Although I was never physically beaten at Fairbridge, we were intimidated by the cottage workers. I yearned for my mother to tell me that she wanted me with her. Instead, she allowed Larissa to go home for the holidays, but not me. I wasn't really surprised; I had known somehow that this would happen. I lived with the knowledge of her constant rejection. Gradually, over the years of my childhood, her behaviour towards me turned me into a depressed and suicidal young girl.

After a year at Fairbridge, Larissa and I joined my mother and our elder sister Sofia at a migrant centre for a few months. Eventually Mum found a unit in Karawara, a small housing estate surrounded by a pine plantation, south of Perth, and we went to live there. Finally we were all together again—and it wasn't long before our former way of life was resumed. Only this time it was worse. Sofia began to use drugs and my younger sister started to hurt herself. She would bang her head against the wall and punch herself black-and-blue. Because I was jealous of the fact that my mother loved Larissa but not me, I added to her injuries by beating her up. My mother would play emotional games with the two of us, turning us against each other at an early age. She would tell Larissa she mustn't talk to me, often for days on end. If Larissa was caught disobeying her, she would be threatened and even locked in a room or cupboard as punishment. Poor Larissa! She suffered enormously because of the situation between my mother and myself. If I thought she was siding with my mother I would beat her, and if she disobeyed Mum then *she* would beat her. Larissa's problems were complex. We were both victims of child abuse.

Larissa and I went to Koonawarra Primary School, in a nearby suburb. I was in Year 6 and Mrs Riberras was our teacher. I loved her. I felt close to her, and I thought that she cared about me as a mother would. I never had the courage to tell her about the abuse at home, but she made the daytime great. I used to steal cheap jewellery from shops to give to her. I wanted to please her all the time and I had a secret fantasy that she might adopt me, but of course it didn't happen. It seemed that the harder I tried to gain love, the more rejected I became. About halfway through that first term, Mrs Riberras started to pay more attention to another girl, Susan, than she did to me, and I was so upset that I ran away. I turned up at home in the evening and my mother told me to get out and stay out. I screamed at her because Larissa was inside and I wanted to come in too, but Mum wouldn't let me. She began to kick me, calling me a little cretin and a slut, and told me she hated me, that she had always hated me. Then she slammed the door in my face. I begged her to give me some food, but there was no response. There never seemed to be enough food at home.

I really couldn't stand living with my mother. Her moods went up and down like an elevator. I think now that she should have sought counselling from a psychiatrist. Our family life was so unhappy. Every weekend I used to go away to friends' places, and sometimes I'd stay with them on week nights as well. I was looking for substitute families who would make me feel wanted. Needless to say, my mother didn't like this. Going to school was my greatest escape from unhappiness. I loved learning—I think I was just about the only kid who didn't wag school regularly.

That night after my mother slammed the door in my face I went to our next-door neighbour and asked to use the toilet. In the bathroom I found a razor, then went off to a building site down the road. As I walked I cried without stopping. When I got there I sat down, ran the razor across my wrists and began to cut. For the first time in my life I felt in control...of the razor and of my life. Many of my confused feelings seem to pour out of me. I felt depressed, but I was in control. For years, ever since I was a tiny kid, even though my parents would beat and abuse me, I used to pretend that I was happy. Then, after my father left, I would fantasise that I had a loving mum. Now, as I cried and cut myself deeper, I felt powerful. I felt that I could control my emotions. When the blood started to run it seemed as though my pain was running out with it. But this didn't last. I knew that if I cut too deep I could die, and I did not want to die. I always wanted to survive, even then.

Eventually I went home again, to receive a mouthful of insults. My mother told me she had put a curse on me. (She was very superstitious.) She had an African voodoo doll which she stuck pins into, and she told me I would feel pain in my body wherever she placed the next pin. I used to believe all the things she said. All she ever did was to bully me into submission. It seemed that everyone I had ever trusted had given me reason to fear them. Practically since the day I was born I had been emotionally, physically and sexually battered. I didn't want this sort of life. It had left me without a shred of self-esteem, just self-hatred. I felt dirty and worthless, and there was a lot of anger hidden away inside me. I remember that on one occasion I saw a little boy about five years old on the building site. He was happy and smiling, and I knew he must have a family who loved him. I was so jealous that I beat him up and locked him in the builders' toilets.

But I never showed my anger properly until I met Lewis, my first boyfriend. This was when I was about fourteen. Lewis went to my school and his family lived very close to us, only nine houses away. Lewis's house became my home and his family became mine. We'd often hang out together till all hours of the night. I really enjoyed walking the streets with Lewis. He wasn't the greatest looking boy, but he had a heart of gold. He had straw-coloured hair and deep blue eyes and he was my first true love.

Living in suburbia was boring for adolescents like us. Lewis and I formed a gang of all the local kids, and we'd spend the nights walking around the neighbourhood pelting cars with eggs and being generally destructive. To begin with I could never actually bring myself to throw an egg—I was too scared my mother would find out. She always seemed to know whenever I did anything wrong. (She told me she was a witch and could find out anything, and I used to believe her.) Then one night Lewis told me to have a go at the egg throwing, and I did. For the first time my anger really came out as I hurled one egg after another. I didn't care if my mother found out and turned me into a voodoo zombie! I was in control now, I could express my feelings.

a ward of the state

⟡

In 1980 I discovered that my mother was privately plotting to have me made a ward of the state. At this time I had been going about with Lewis and the neighbourhood gang for about three months. When I came home from school one day, my mum accused me of burgling a neighbour's house. She telephoned the police and sent me to my room. Two police officers arrived and she invited them in. She encouraged them to tell me that if I didn't behave they would lock me up in prison, and they went along with this. I was scared, but I was also confused: here was my mother, who had abused me for years, pointing me out as a criminal—and the police wouldn't even listen to what I had to say. While they were reprimanding me and making me feel like *I* was the criminal, I broke down. I grabbed a razor blade and ran out of the house, telling them I was going to kill myself. My mother, calling me a thief and an attention seeker, yelled out to me to go ahead and make sure I did it properly.

There wasn't really anywhere to run to, so I went and sat on the ground at the building site. I hoped the police would find me, so that I could tell them what my life had been like all these years, but they never came. As I sat contemplating suicide I began to feel more and more angry—too angry to die. I didn't want to die, I wanted to experience the good in life. I knew it was out there somewhere.

After this the situation at home went from bad to worse. As soon as I came home from school Mum would start swearing at me, telling me how rotten I was. I would swear back at her, then she would pin me against the wall with her hands around my throat, threatening to have me locked away in prison. This was her latest weapon. One day, as she pushed at me, the bubble of repressed anger and resentment that had been boiling inside me for over ten years finally burst. We were in the kitchen—I picked up a fork and lunged at her. I wanted to kill her for all those years of emotional abuse … but I couldn't. Yet for the first time in my life, in the midst of a confrontation with her, I felt in control instead of overcome by her threats. After a brief struggle I dropped the fork and ran out. "You fucking little evil slut, we curse you!" she screamed after me. The African voodoo doll was lying on the kitchen table. "See this doll? We curse you and you will die!" And she stuck a pin through the doll's heart.

I knew my mother would get on the phone to the police straight away, so I had to run away. I went down to my friend Samantha's house, in the next street, and told her what I had done and what my mother had said. I was terrified of my mother's curse—she had told me that two people had died from her curses, and I believed her. I was scared stiff. I convinced Sam that I had to run away, and asked her to help me. She said she wanted to come with me, because she was sad that my family were so mean to me.

Samantha took all the money out of her piggy-bank and we bundled up a tent that belonged to her parents, and helped ourselves to canned food out of the cupboard. Then we walked into the Karawara pine forest and set up camp. It was really scary. We'd forgotten the can-opener and soon it began to get dark and we shivered with cold. I for one was having second thoughts about running away from home. I told Samantha I would have to go back and face the music. My mother would have contacted the police, and they would be looking for both of us. Samantha said that having plucked up the courage to run away, she was too frightened to return. As I set off I told her I would come back to see her in the morning.

At home I found my mother hysterical, but not on my account. She said I'd given her a bad name. Samantha's father was there, and he begged me to tell him where his daughter was. He was really worried about her. I told him she was camping, and wanted to stay out until the morning. He was an understanding man; he didn't shout at me, he just said a few sensible words and left. After he'd gone, my mum screamed at me and said that now I had finally proved to everyone I was the rotten kid she always knew I was. She called the Victoria Park police, and told them just how uncontrollable I was. The police told her that they couldn't take me in unless I had committed some serious crime. I hadn't, of course, but she went on and on, saying that being uncontrollable was a crime and a good reason why I should be locked up. Then she told them I had threatened to take her life. Finally she persuaded them to come to the house. The police dragged me downstairs by my hair, handcuffs were placed on me, and I was put into a locked police van. My mother's plan to have me made a ward of the state was set in motion. My road to hell was beginning.

I was driven to Longmore, a maximum detention centre for boys and girls, and put on remand for being uncontrollable. No one ever asked me why I had acted the way I did, nor why I so often wet my bed. I knew it was going to be a long road for me.

As soon as I arrived I was ordered to strip and bend over in front of a staff member—they were looking for concealed drugs and checking for venereal disease. It was humiliating to have to do all this with a complete stranger perving on me. Then I was given some head-lice shampoo and ordered to shower and wash my hair. After this I was placed in a detention room the size of a shoe-box. I was told to sleep on the floor. Well, at that point anything was better than being at home.

After a week at Longmore I had to attend the court hearing where my mother applied to have me made a ward of the state. She stood in the courtroom and told the magistrate how utterly uncontrollable I was. She said she had tried her very best to look after me, but I was a thoroughly evil child and she just couldn't cope with my violence any longer. There was no mention of her emotional and physical abuse of me. The hearing was one big farce, a conspiracy against me. When the magistrate asked my mother what she thought should be done with me, she replied that the only solution was to make me a ward of the state and lock me away. She said no one else would want me—and she was right. So it was decided: I became a ward of the state.

I was taken straight from the Magistrate's Court to Mount Lawley Receiving Home. It was far worse than Longmore. At Mount Lawley I was constantly sexually harassed, touched and mauled by the older boys there, while the staff turned a blind eye. Once, in the classroom, a boy about sixteen pinned me down, held a butter knife at my throat, and tried to have sex with me. I was screaming my head off, but the teacher just laughed and looked away. No one cared. Inmates at Mount Lawley were issued with garments from a clothing pool. If they were ten sizes too big that was just tough luck. I got the impression that no one at this Government children's home gave a stuff about the kids or how they behaved; all they were worried about was getting the weekly pay-cheque.

A girl called Monique, whom I .had known at Fairbridge Farm School, was at Mount Lawley. We became good friends in spite of the difference in our ages—she was seventeen and I was only thirteen. Monique told me she was sick of being badly treated, and had made up her mind to run away from Mount Lawley. I asked if I could go with her. She was hesitant at first, but finally she decided it might be fun to go together; the only condition she made was that I must pay my own way.

Monique planned to escape after breakfast one morning. On the chosen day, I woke up early, had a shower, then headed to the clothing pool. I didn't want to leave wearing the awful dress I had on. I asked the staff member in charge if l could have a pair of jeans, but she threw another dress at me. When I complained, she said I was being cheeky and made me sweep and mop the kitchen. This took a fair bit of time, and I knew that Monique didn't want to delay. I went up to Mary, an Aboriginal girl about my size, and asked her if she would swap clothes with me. She gave me her jeans and jumper, which I hastily put on, then fled to join Monique, who was waiting for me across the road outside the Home. To tell the truth, I really hated running away. I always yearned for stability in my life—and a loving family. Yet while I went on searching for these things, other kids were craving more freedom.

Monique and I didn't stay together for long. She decided to go off to her boyfriend's place. She told me he was a heroin addict, and I felt uncomfortable when I heard that. Instead, I decided to find my own boyfriend, Lewis, and I headed off alone into the city. Lewis had left the suburbs and gone to live there with some of his friends. Although he had a home and family, he rarely saw them these days. It was great being with him again. He always made me feel safe, and I trusted him. Now he told me that. he wanted to stay with me and take care of me. We would be on the run together.

We decided we needed some money. We walked around town, went into a few shops, and finally reached a jewellery store in Adelaide Terrace. There was a middle-aged woman behind the counter, which displayed a collection of small, solid gold nuggets—the city had a goldfields and bush ranger promotional theme that week. I asked to look at some rings. While I was doing this, the woman turned to speak to Lewis. Impulsively I reached across the counter, grabbed a handful of the gold nuggets and screamed out to Lewis to run like hell. We didn't stop running until we reached the other side of town. I felt guilty, but I knew we needed money. Now we wondered how we could convert the nuggets into cash.

We backtracked towards the city and walked through the busy Hay Street Mall. Suddenly I spotted a sign outside a menswear shop: WE WILL BUY ALL YOUR GOLD THIS WEEK. The shop was running some sort of scheme to tie in with the promotional theme. I told Lewis to wait outside and walked into the shop, where I approached the sales assistant. "Excuse me, sir," I said, holding out my handful of nuggets, "I'd like to sell this gold. My father and I found it on a fossicking expedition to Kalgoorlie." I don't know why the hell he believed me, maybe it was my angel face, but he offered me $250 for the gold. I decided it was a fair price, pocketed the money and quickly left the shop.

I told Lewis it was crazy for us to stick together all the time. The police knew he was my boyfriend, and I didn't want to be caught and taken back to Longmore. I was petrified of ending up back there. So we parted for the time being, and I decided to visit a few pinball hang-outs in the Mall. I met up with Gloria, an Aboriginal girl I'd talked to on the streets before. She told me some other girls were after her and she was afraid they'd find her here, so we walked to the other end of town. I told Gloria I was going to see someone I knew who owned a shop in London Court Arcade. This guy, Serge, was always trying to chat me up, even though he was too old for me, about forty-five. But I thought he might agree to help us to book into a hotel. We both looked too young to do this ourselves—the desk clerk would be suspicious. When we reached his shop, he agreed to help us, on condition that we went back to his place for a drink. Gloria looked dubious, but I told her we would only stay with him for an hour or so, then leave.

What happened was that Serge locked the door of his

unit, grabbed Gloria by the hair and raped her. I tried to stop him, but he began to threaten me. I didn't know what to do. I couldn't call the police. Finally I picked up a knife, told him to leave Gloria alone, and we escaped. After this we decided we should buy a couple of knives for protection, and went along to the Girl Guides shop, where I bought two pocket knives. That was a horrible episode for Gloria. I understood what she'd been through, but didn't know how to help her. She asked me what we were going to do now, and I said I'd get a hotel room somehow.

We walked back to the city and chatted up a guy in the Mall. He was drunk. I offered him twenty dollars to book us a room and tell the hotel manager we were his cousins. The manager took our money and showed us to a room, where we got drunk and stoned, and then passed out.

Around midnight I woke suddenly. The door was open and four torches were shining on my face. The police had arrived. One officer pulled the blankets off the bed and told Gloria to get up. We both stood there in our bras and pants. I was angry that the mongrel hotel manager had taken our money then called the police. The coppers allowed us five minutes to get dressed, then handcuffed us and threw us into a divvy van stinking of vomit and urine. They gave no explanation of their actions.

As I walked into Perth Central police station I got a real shock. The police were interviewing and interrogating Lewis. I was taken alone into a separate room where they began to interrogate me as well. One of the officers ordered me to stand in the corner with my hands raised above my head; he kept me there for forty minutes, the bastard. Then he told me that Lewis had admitted everything and that it was no good lying to them because they already had a statement from him. It was all made up—Lewis hadn't confessed, it was a trick to make me tell them the truth. But I believed it. I made my confession and signed a statement, after which they decided it would be fun to make me hold a telephone book above my head for an hour. I despised those cops—I still do. (Years later, I heard that one of them ended up in prison himself, which seemed to prove that what goes around, comes around.)

After this, Gloria and I were taken to the East Perth lockup, where we were fingerprinted, photographed and strip-searched before being thrown into the stinking cells. We stayed there for six hours until the staff at Longmore were contacted, and we were driven to the Home in a paddy wagon. I remember the fun the cops had during that journey. They pulled up somewhere in Bentley, where they got out and began to rock the van, laughing and telling us they'd love to rape us. I was extremely scared. I hated being treated as though I was a criminal. Even though I had stolen those nuggets, I did not feel like a criminal. I felt more like a hurt child.

At Longmore, Gloria and I were separated. I was put in the holding cells, where I went to sleep, hungry and terrified, on the concrete floor. I dreaded what the next day would bring. In fact, running away from Mount Lawley was one of the biggest mistakes of my life. Later, at a case conference, I learned that the authorities had planned for me to live in a family setting in the suburb of Nedlands. I had ruined a chance to live a normal life.

In the morning the police arrived about seven o'clock and took me off to the East Perth Children's Court. My mother was there, and she managed to convince everyone I was the most evil child who ever walked the earth. She told the court I was a dangerous influence and had led my younger sister astray. To me it seemed unbelievable that the court accepted her words. Couldn't they see that I was the victim, not my mother? I managed to scream out to the magistrate that Mum had been abusing me for years, but he just told me that I was a rude girl, and that he would put me in contempt of court unless I stopped shouting. It was all hopeless. The court had decided I was guilty. The magistrate ordered that I was to be put under the care and control of Nyandi Treatment and Research Centre for Delinquents until I was eighteen years of age. Eighteen. I faced four years of imprisonment and punishment.

nyandi

✍

To describe Nyandi as a "home" would be very far from the true meaning of that word. Nyandi was designed to be sheer hell for its inmates. It began as soon as I arrived. The only greeting I received was: "Now, you do as we say—or else". I was taken to a small, solitary room and ordered to strip, squat and bend over in front of two staff members. Then they watched me shower, and threw me a dress and a pair of paper underpants. After that I was led into a narrow passageway, where I was told to sit down at a desk facing the blank wall. They said I was to stay there until I was told otherwise. A youth worker appeared; he introduced himself as Peter. He told me I was in "Time-out" and that I wasn't allowed to move, talk or do anything other than sit there facing the wall. This was something my mother used to do to me: I felt as if I had been punished this way forever, that history was repeating itself. Of all the punishments at Nyandi, I hated Time-out the most.

At the end of the afternoon I was led into the main area of the building, known as Pineview. Nyandi was really very small—apart from the staff quarters and dormitories there were just four small rooms, a lounge and dining area, and the dreaded Time-out passageway. At one end of the building there was a small swimming pool, rarely used, and a grassed courtyard surrounded by a high brick wall. Nyandi wasn't really a treatment centre at all. The staff wore white coats and we were the guinea pigs.

As soon as we awoke each day, we were programmed to conform to Nyandi's strict and rigid rules. We were issued with a behaviour-monitoring sheet every morning, listing twenty or so examples of "good behaviour." Each time we performed one of these we earned twenty points, while for every one not performed we lost 100 points. One example on the list was "Care and Concern." If, for instance, you made a staff member a cup of tea, you earned your twenty points under this heading. The result was that the girls ended up competing for who would make each staff member a cup of tea. While we suffered the staff were pampered.

To begin with, I spent most of my time at Nyandi in Time-out. I would sit facing the wall for hours, sometimes days, even weeks at a time. There were no magazines and I wasn't allowed to talk to anyone—if I did, I got more time. It felt like I spent years in Time-out. I'd be woken at six-thirty in the morning and had to sit at that desk all day until nine at night. Fourteen hours straight, day in, day out. When you were in Time-out you were also punished with solitary confinement in locked rooms which I called the cells. They had a toilet and shower and a bed with a solid iron frame. There was a small plastic window the staff could look through. The whole concept of Time-out combined with solitary confinement was emotionally destructive and barbaric rather than helpful.

I am convinced that if the kids at Nyandi had been shown real care and kindness, if the staff had talked to them properly instead of isolating them, that would have gone a lot further than such continuous punishment. Almost every day some incident occurred which resulted in me being dragged kicking and screaming into solitary confinement. The system of Time-out also neglected the nutritional needs of the kids at Nyandi. We were given a slice of toast and a glass of milk for breakfast, a Vegemite sandwich and a glass of milk for lunch, and dinner at night was also a joke. The staff made sure that the size of our meals was part of the psychological punishment they inflicted on us.

Nyandi just could not deal with me. The staff never sat down to try to figure out what was wrong with me, why I behaved the way I did. I had been abused throughout my childhood, and they simply did not care. It was after my third month at Nyandi that I began to cut myself on a regular basis. One afternoon, at the end of our daily lessons in the schoolroom, I pushed the alarm bell intentionally, so that they would put me back into Time-out. (There were alarm bells all over the building.) After the bell sounded, two staff members came running down to the schoolroom and dragged me out by my arms and hair, then threw me into a solitary cell. I knew that if I'd asked to go there voluntarily, they would not have allowed it. This cell was barely big enough to lie down in. It contained nothing and was completely dark except for a peephole. It was almost like a coffin. The light switch was on the outside—I was left alone in that terrifying darkness. But I had stolen a pencil sharpener from the schoolroom and hidden it down my pants. This was all part of my plan. I took out the pencil sharpener and began to cut myself with its blade. The more I cut the more anger I expressed—and once again I felt I was in control. After this, cutting myself became a daily ritual, allowing me to go on feeling as though I was in control.

After I was released from the cell I was given further punishment for cutting myself. The staff didn't really care about any of us; they came and went and never got to know us properly. I was just a big problem that they hated. There was no escape from the cycle of misbehaviour and punishment—the worse I behaved, the harder it got for me. I sank into a deep depression, spending most of my time alone, cutting myself and hiding the slash marks from the staff.

Then, having completed my initial three months in custody, I was told I was being sent over to Gwynne-Lea Cottage to finish my program. Gwynne-Lea was called a hostel, but it was really just an extension to Nyandi, situated across the road. I wasn't excited about going there because it meant I had to leave Robyn, the only friend I'd made at Nyandi. And I knew that the staff would still throw me into solitary confinement if I didn't behave. I was right. The staff at Gwynne-Lea took a dislike to me from the moment I arrived there. They soon decided I wasn't conforming like the other kids, so they called Nyandi. Someone promptly appeared and dragged me back into a cell. I was told I would remain permanently in Time-out until they could work out what to do with me. I felt as if I was a piece of garbage being tossed about.

Finally I was called into the office and informed that I would be kept in permanent isolation at Nyandi, but that I would be allowed to attend Perth Modern High School. I was ecstatic! But I was careful not to show it, because I knew that if they saw my delight they would take it away from me. For the first night in three months I didn't cut myself. I hugged my pillow and went straight to sleep. But my excitement was dampened when they told me I was to join a special class at the school so that my behaviour could be monitored. I would have to take a behaviour-monitoring card to school each day, which had to be signed after each lesson. I felt humiliated by this. All I wanted was to be treated like a normal schoolgirl, but it seemed that would never happen.

In spite of this, I really loved Perth Modern High School. I had a fantastic teacher, Mr Bill Helm, who was great with the kids. Every day I looked forward to going to school because he made it such fun. He always respected us. Sometimes we went on outings. I built up good friendships with all the kids in my class. My best friend at school was Rebecca. She had red hair and so much talent. We became best mates and hung out together all the time. I found it was hard to cope with spending such wonderful days at school, then coming back to Nyandi and its points system for good behaviour. I was also being picked on and tormented by two girls at Nyandi who were deeply jealous of the fact that I was allowed to go to school. They were always threatening me and made my life there even more hellish. There was no escape from them, so I began to cut myself again. One of them, Jaylene, was a sixteen-year-old Aboriginal girl, a real standover. One day she threatened to kill me if I didn't buy her some cigarettes. She gave me the money to do this. I didn't have any choice, so I bought her what she wanted and hid the contraband in the bottom of my schoolbag. But when I came back from school that same afternoon, one of the staff told me that I was to be searched. Of course she found the stuff in my bag and took me straight to Time-out. After that I was told I would not be going back to school. Jaylene and her friend ended up getting their cigarettes from visitors who came to see them, so my smuggling effort, for which I had to pay dearly, had all been in vain.

During my time in Nyandi my mother occasionally came to visit me, and she used to bring her pet rat with her. Some of the staff thought she was mad, and for some reason I found myself defending her. I don't know why. Yet I knew that I still wanted her love, which she had always refused me.

Meanwhile, during a routine health check at school, the visiting doctor had discovered that I had developed severe scoliosis, curvature of the spine. I had an appointment to see a specialist at the Royal Perth Rehabilitation Hospital, and arrangements were made for my mother to attend as well as two of the staff from Nyandi. The specialist told me that I needed immediate surgery to prevent further damage to my spine. I was then taken back to Nyandi to await the operation. My mother had shown no concern for me during the interview with the specialist. There never, ever, seemed any love in my world. I had never been hugged or praised, just threatened, abused and punished. I wondered when it would all end.

I was taken to the Sir Charles Gardener Hospital for tests, to see whether my body could cope with the operation. Two staff members from Nyandi came with me to make sure I didn't abscond. Within two weeks I was admitted to hospital, and Nyandi sent a female staff member to sit beside me day and night. I could not understand why I needed guarding—I knew perfectly well that I had to have this operation; it was for my own good. I kicked up a huge fuss and said I wouldn't go through with it if I was to be guarded all the time. An hour later the staff member went and I was left in the sole charge of the nurses. However, as I found out later, the reason she left wasn't because of the fuss I'd made, but because Nyandi had decided it was a waste of money.

The operation was very painful, and I remained in intensive care for two weeks. That was the worst time. The nurses used to turn me over on a striker bed. The entire length of my back had been cut and there was a metal rod all the way down my spine. It was called the Harrington Rod operation. I also had a bone graft, and for six weeks I had to lie flat on my back. I wasn't allowed to move. My only conversations were with the old people in the ward—most of them talked all the time about their bowel surgery or their piles. It made me feel very depressed. I asked if I could be placed in a ward with some other kids, but I was told there weren't any vacant beds, so instead I went into a private room. I only had two visitors—Theresa, my after-care officer, and my mother. They came only once, and they arrived together. I really liked Theresa a lot, but I couldn't talk to her properly with my mother there. As it was lunch time, the nurses asked my mother if she would feed me, since I was unable to feed myself at that stage. She refused, so Theresa fed me instead. Small things like that seemed to reaffirm the hatred my mother felt for me. Part of me never wanted to see her again, but another part was desperate for her love. I hung on, hoping...

When the six weeks were up I had a plaster cast that reached from my neck down to my hips wrapped around me. I was supposed to wear this for a year. As it was midsummer, it was very uncomfortable. I wasn't allowed to shower for a further three months, since the plaster had to stay dry, so I really suffered.

I do have one pleasant memory of being in hospital. After the operation, when I was able to walk about, I met a girl about my age whose name was Roxanne. She was very pretty and had a lovely family who always came to visit her. I envied her and wished I was like her, and it was then that I decided to call myself "Roxanne" instead of Elizabeth, a name which I had never liked.

Eventually I was released from hospital in my plaster cast—I was picked up by two of the youth workers who drove me back to Nyandi, where I was put into Pineview, the main area. I was in a room with two other girls and I got on with them really well. I asked the staff if I would be going back to school, but they told me I had ruined my chances and was a stupid bitch for having tried to smuggle in the cigarettes. I said that I hoped they might change their minds; I pointed out that I could have run away from the hospital during the last few days I was there, but I hadn't done so.

Robyn, my best friend, was in Pineview as well, and we hung out together. I loved Robyn, she was the only person I could really talk to. We were inseparable. The staff didn't like it when any of the girls formed close friendships, and they thought that Robyn and I were a bad influence on each other. They were always trying to separate us. I think they felt that because we were so close to each other, we were undermining their control.

In the end the staff decided I was allowed to go back to Perth Modern High School after all. I was to be strip searched when I returned each day, and I wasn't allowed any money for lunches, in case I bought smokes and bolt cutters to bring back for the other inmates. I wasn't allowed to go on any excursions without special permission, nor to take part in any after-school activities, or visit school friends' houses. If I broke any of these conditions, I would remain in isolation and be banned from school once and for all.

Once again Jaylene pressured me to buy cigarettes. I was scared, but I had no choice. At school I asked Rebecca if she would lend me ten dollars, which she did. I got the cigarettes from a newsagent's. There was a chemist's shop next door, and on a sudden impulse I went in and bought a packet of non-prescriptive sleeping pills called Sedu-caps. I stuffed everything down my plaster as far as I could. When I was searched on my return the Nyandi staff missed the contraband this time. I gave the cigarettes to the girls and spent the rest of the night worrying in case they would get me to bring things in every day. I wasn't a very happy girl most of the time—I used to go about with a permanent scowl on my face. There was deep hurt and deep anger inside me. I seemed always to have felt that way.

The next day Jaylene and some of the other girls were caught smoking—the smoke made the fire alarms go off— and they told the staff that I had brought in the cigarettes for them. I was immediately dragged off to Time-out. "I hate you, all of you, you're all bastards. God, please let me die!" I screamed. The staff took me to cabin 11, the worst room in solitary. I knew I wouldn't be allowed to go back to school, which was the only thing that made life bearable for me. Then I remembered that the sleeping pills were still stuffed down my plaster, and I vowed to swallow every one of them. I asked for a drink of water, but this was refused. I reached into my plaster, took out the pills and managed to swallow them all without any water. Within five minutes everything went black. Dimly I recall Daryl, one of the youth workers, trying to get me to stand up—it was impossible. He wanted to make me walk, but I kept falling down. The pills were knocking me out. He slapped me hard across my face in a final attempt to revive me, and I passed out.

This was my first overdose. I knew nothing more until I came to in hospital, where the nurses and doctors were forcing tubes into my stomach, and I realised I wasn't going to die after all. I was relieved, but I knew that I would be punished when I got back to Nyandi. I felt completely exhausted and stayed in hospital overnight. The Nyandi staff were told that I should receive counselling, and they agreed to this. But nothing happened: instead, I was dragged back into Time-out. So much for counselling. The staff totally ignored me—I was back at the wall for forty eight hours.

Finally I realised that my existence here was totally un-acceptable. Somehow I gathered inner strength and decided that I was not going to let them overcome me every day. I was continually asked if I was sorry about what I'd done; I was told that until I said I was sorry, I would do more time. I was sick of being emotionally battered. I was determined not to give in.

There were some staff members at Nyandi I genuinely liked, but the system never allowed them to become personally involved with any of us, or to show concern or care. They were employed to carry out the rules, and that is what they did. One staff member, Paul, was my favourite. He was the softest person and tried to be nice to us, but the rules forbade his good intention. The funny thing was that when I felt good and mad I would take out my anger on poor Paul. I think I always tried to hurt those who cared about me, because by this time I was too wary of allowing people to get close to me.

Robert, a psychologist, finally came to see me. I asked him if I would be able to go back to school. He was really nice, but he said it wasn't in his power to make a decision about that.

It was up to my new after-care officer. I knew she would never let me go back—she was the hard sort, a real bitch type, not a bit like Theresa. So I asked if I could go back to Pineview, to be with the other kids. Robert talked to the staff and they decided I could. It was good to be able to talk to Robyn; we spent most of our time making great plans for when we both got out. While I was in solitary confinement I used to fantasise about having a loving family. I often dreamt that I was really loved and I hung on to those dreams. I told myself that one day they would come true.

Life in Nyandi was extremely artificial. We were surrounded by barred windows, fluorescent lights and high walls. Even though I hated and despised the Nyandi system, over a period of time I began to feel safe inside it, and started to think of ways to stay there. Now that I was back in Pineview, things were a little better, but I still felt deeply depressed. I walked about with an inner feeling of dread and had no idea how to cope with it.

One afternoon a male youth worker was on duty who really loathed me. Every time he appeared I seemed to freak out. He ordered me to wash and dry-up after lunch, and I accidentally dropped a plate. "Okay, Roxanne, off to Time out," he said. (The staff and everyone else had got used to using my new name by now). I managed to pick up a piece of the broken plate in the ensuing struggle, and he threw me into one of the cells. He ripped off my clothes and held me down until I thought I would choke. Finally he left, slamming the metal door behind him. Slowly I began to cut myself. With each cut I would utter a cry of frustration and pain. I was really hurting inside. I don't know why hurting myself physically made me feel better, but it did. I think I was so used to being abused that to hurt myself seemed normal. I was left in solitary for three hours, then returned to my bedroom. I still felt total anger: I wanted to get back at them for punishing me for no reason. I jumped in the shower and spent the next two hours ripping off my plaster. I knew this would make them angry. I heard Daryl, another of the youth workers, call my name. He unlocked the door and looked into the shower. By that time everything was covered in pieces of plaster. He ran out and called the doctor, who told the staff to wrap bandages around me until next morning, when an ambulance took me to hospital. I received no sympathy, but then I didn't expect any.

After I was admitted to hospital, Gordon, the staff member who accompanied me there, told me that I would be guarded so that I wouldn't abscond. For me this was the final straw. Why did they always treat me like a criminal? I asked Gordon if I could get up to go to the toilet, and he said no. In fact, I wasn't supposed to get up until I was given a new plaster cast. I picked up a tumbler on the bedside locker and smashed it, then began to slash at myself with a shard of glass. Blood poured from my arm as Gordon screamed for a doctor. The doctor ran in and while I was held down he stitched my arm and injected me with a sedative.

I floated in and out of sleep. Maybe I was tackling my misery the wrong way, but I couldn't think of any other way to cope with the mess I was in. After the sedative wore off it was time for Gordon to go home. He told me that Peter was the next worker on duty. Peter was one of the worst, very strict, and I think he hated me as much as I hated him. I dropped off to sleep once more, and when I woke up I saw that he had arrived. I asked him for a book, but he said I wasn't getting a thing after the way I had behaved, and as far as he was concerned I could stay on the bed forever. I looked around the room and saw that he had taken everything away. Once again I was in prison. I knew I had to do something. I just couldn't stand it any more.

I got out of bed in a sudden rush, ran over to the window, opened it and jumped out. It was two storeys high and I really thought I would damage myself quite badly. After all, it was only a few months since I'd had major spinal surgery and a bone graft. The rod inside my back could easily have snapped. But I managed to get up from the ground and then I began to run for my life. It felt so strange, running without the support of my plaster cast, it was almost like floating. The cast had been so heavy. I went across the road outside the hospital—I remember there was a woman working in her garden. I heard shouts and looked behind to see two nurses, a doctor and a couple of orderlies chasing after me. Then I heard an ambulance siren. The ambulance was following me. The more they shouted at me to stop, the more determined I felt to get away from Nyandi and all the people who went on and on ill-treating me.

One of the nurses had almost caught up with me. I panicked. I picked up a garden fork from someone's front garden and turned to face my pursuers. I told them that if they came any closer I would fight them. The doctor tried to calm me, but I was spilling over with anger. Deep down, I was also sick with worry about the punishment I would receive once this was all over. Inside, I was just a scared kid crying out to be loved, but I had built a wall around me about six bricks thick. I didn't really want to hurt anyone, but I was sick of being dominated and controlled. All I wanted was to be in control of myself. Now I felt trapped: there was no escape. I told the doctor that if he came any closer I would kill someone. He tried his hardest to contain the situation, telling me that I wouldn't be punished, that he was worried about me and the damage I was doing to my spine. He told me that if I kept walking without my plaster I could end up dislodging the rod and pins. Something inside me told me to listen to his words—maybe it was the unusually caring tone in his voice. Certainly I didn't want to end up a cripple. I told him I would put down the garden fork and return to the hospital so long as Peter left me alone.

As we stood there in the street, the police arrived, then left.

I realised I couldn't go on standing there all day. By this time a small crowd of onlookers had gathered. I had to give myself up. I got into the ambulance and one of the nurses talked to me until we reached the hospital. I stayed there for three days, I was given my new plaster and then they set me back to Nyandi. What would happen now? Graham, the psychologist, told me I was going to Watson Lodge, a hostel at Northbridge run by Nyandi staff.

After I arrived there I found out that Robyn had left Nyandi; she was now living in South Perth. I telephoned her and we arranged to meet in Fremantle. I managed to walk out of Watson Lodge without too much difficulty, but I knew the staff there would call the police as soon as they discovered I was missing. Even if I returned voluntarily I knew they would send me back to Nyandi.

Now I was really on the run.

street kid

❧

Robyn and I, both runaways, knew we would have to steal in order to survive. We took food and clothes from the super- markets and lived on the streets. It was a fairly perilous form of existence, and eventually we got sick of it. We had a very close friendship, and we made a pact never to go off and do anything alone, but always to stick together. One day we decided we would both take an overdose. We went to a chemist, bought heaps of pills, then sat in Fremantle Park and swallowed the lot. Although they weren't prescription drugs, we knew it was dangerous to take too many of them. Next thing we knew we woke up in Fremantle Hospital. We had succeeded in carrying out our pact, but the fact that we were so sick and felt so awful made it seem more like failure.

As the doctors and nurses attended to us, I felt a sense of being cared for, of being looked after, and I think Robyn did too. As it turned out we hadn't swallowed a dangerous amount of tablets, but the hospital kept us in for observation. I felt secure in hospital—and no one was punishing me. I told the psychiatrist who came to see us that I took the overdose because I was stressed. He gave me a prescription for a sedative called Normison. After that experience we went on taking overdoses—maybe, subconsciously, we knew it was the only way we could get the attention we had both craved for so long. The really scary thing was that we would go to such extraordinary lengths just to feel wanted.

One morning as Robyn and I walked around Fremantle, she dared me to steal some clothes from K-Mart. We would always tempt each other to do stupid things—it was like a game and provided some excitement. I nicked some jeans and a T-shirt and after I left the store we headed for the bus stop. As we sat there talking, I heard someone shout out my name: "Roxanne!" The next moment Ian, one of the youth workers from Nyandi, was grabbing my arm. He was very strong and as I struggled I screamed out: "Rape! Help!" A few people tried to tackle him, ignoring the words he blurted out: "She's a runaway from Nyandi Centre!" It was the funniest sight—all those people holding him down, believing he was trying to attack us. I hope someone called the police to arrest him! Then a bus heading for Perth came along and Robyn screamed at me to jump on it.

My relationship with Robyn was the closest I had known with anyone—we never fought or argued. The perfect friendship. We were always aware that the police were looking for us and once again we decided to seek the care and safety of being in hospital. We spent the rest of our money on different kinds of pills, mostly sedatives, then went to a park close by the Royal Perth Hospital, where we swallowed two handfuls each. There were about 150 altogether. Once again, I awoke with tubes in my arms, a long tube down my nose, and a heart monitor beside my bed. As one nurse wiped my forehead I heard another say: "It's her again". I tried to talk, but the words wouldn't come. I was really scared that I had gone too far this time. I drifted in and out of consciousness, trying to work out what was happening, but my mind was completely spaced out.

I finally came to and was able to ask a nurse whether Robyn was okay. The nurse told me Robyn was in intensive care. She said I would pull through all right, but Robyn was very sick. I was absolutely terrified. We must have taken too many pills, and I blamed myself. If Robyn died it would be my fault. I vowed never to do it again.

Robyn didn't die, but the doctors wanted her to stay in hospital because they were worried about possible kidney damage. Seeing her lying there in bed shocked me. She looked so yellow. I had been told I could leave, but that I had to see a hospital social worker first. I said goodbye to Robyn and told her I would call her sister's place to find out how she was.

Then I saw the social worker, he seemed genuinely concerned about me. He asked about my parents and wanted to know how old I was. I managed to convince him I was eighteen (my real age was fourteen). He told me the only thing he could do was to call one of the local hostels to see if I could stay there. I didn't like that idea, so then he suggested that a friend of his called Barry, a Christian social worker, should come to see me. I agreed—I really didn't have a choice, for I knew the police would arrest me if they saw me on the streets.

Barry wasn't the sort of strait-laced Christian I had been expecting. He told me he had served time in prison and had reformed after bringing Jesus into his life. He repeated the suggestion that I should go to one of the local hostels and offered to drive me there. But again I refused, so he gave me his card and left.

Still feeling quite sick from the overdose, I wandered about the city. I felt very alone, a little girl lost, and kept wondering why and how my life had become such a mess. I longed to be somewhere I would feel safe. I went inside a telephone box and looked through the "Help" section in the phone book, but there seemed nowhere to go. I decided to return to Fremantle—at least I would be near Robyn there, once she left hospital. But when I got there I decided I'd had enough. I really hated my day-to-day existence on the streets. I longed for security... three meals a day and Mum, something it seemed I could never have. I returned to Perth, and back at the park, in spite of my recent vow, and my fright at seeing Robyn looking so ill, I decided to slash my wrists and take all my Normison pills. I knew they would knock me out completely because I still had drugs in my body from the last overdose.

Within four minutes everything went black. Once again I came round in hospital, where one of the doctors recognised me from my time at Fremantle Hospital. There was a police officer by my bed. The police had found me slumped beside a tree and thought I had been assaulted. The officer asked my name and I tried to remember the name I had given at Fremantle. "Lisa" I whispered. After a brief lecture on the dangers of drug taking, he left.

I had stitches in my arm and they were throbbing, but the hurt I felt inside was worse than the physical pain. I saw the hospital psychiatrist, who told me he was really worried about the way I kept inflicting damage on myself. I had built up such an emotional barrier around myself that I found it impossible to tell him the truth about my life, about the things that had happened at home. By this time my life seemed to have turned into one battle after another—I had lost sight of the larger picture.

When the psychiatrist told me he was going to commit me to a psychiatric hospital called Heathcote, I was terrified. I'd heard horror stories about the things that went on there. I begged him to change his mind, but he told me it was for the best. I said that if I had to go, I preferred to go voluntarily, and I told him that a friend would take me there. I then telephoned Barry, who spoke to the doctor and agreed to pick me up. When Barry arrived I was sure I'd be able to persuade him to drop me off in town—after all, he'd been in prison himself, he was cool. But when I asked him to let me out of the car he refused. I couldn't believe he really meant to take me to Heathcote, that hell-house. I began to cry, begging him not to take me there, and then, as we came to an intersection, I opened the car door and made a jump for it. Barry drove around the corner and pulled up—we were right opposite police headquarters, and I knew that in ten seconds the police would be out searching for me. I hid behind some bushes at the side of the building, but a cop spotted me. I knew it was all up, and bursting with anger I grabbed a bottle lying on the pavement, smashed it, then slashed my arm. The policeman chasing after me looked quite shocked and called out that everything would be all right. Something in his voice calmed me down, and I held his hand as we went into the police station.

I had no idea why I continually damaged myself—hurting myself just seemed the easiest way of coping with the torment inside me. Inside the station I began crying and screamed out for my "Aunty" Lillian, who was a detective in the Child Protection Unit at police head quarters. She wasn't a real aunty, of course, but she was always there for me when I was in trouble. I had met her the previous year, and she had taken an interest in me and tried her best to help me. She was the only police woman I had met who really cared about the children she came across in her work. When she appeared, I begged her to take me on to Heathcote—I knew I would be all right if I was with her. So after an ambulance paramedic had stitched my arm, Lillian I set off for Heathcote together, and after I was admitted she said goodbye with a hug.

My brief time in Heathcote was sheer hell. The building was out of the last century and the staff seemed even more crazy than the patients. Luckily, however, it was decided this was an unsuitable place for me (maybe Lillian had revealed my true age to the authorities) and I was released the next day.

I had no idea where to go, and in the end I decided to visit Barry. I had his card, and knew that he shared with a flatmate called John. I arrived at his place, walked up to the apartment, and discovered Barry wasn't at home. John was there, however, and he asked me in. I was surprised to discover how old John was. He had a rough manner, but somehow it was easy to talk to him. He seemed nice. I told him everything, that I was a runaway and had been living on the streets, and had ended up being taken to Heathcote. John asked me if I wanted a bed for the night and I accepted. I was so tired, so sick, and so hungry. John cooked a good stew and we sat up talking most of the night. In the morning I left early.

The life of a street kid is simply survival from day to day. By this time I was beginning to feel desperate, and I thumbed a lift to Nedlands, a posh suburb where my elder sister, Sofia, used to share a house with some of her student friends at university. She had a lot of friends and they were like one big family for me. I learned a lot about life from them. At this time Sofia was no longer there, but I went to stay with one of her friends, Rob. He was about thirty and gay, a kind and gentle person. I stayed with Rob for about two weeks, but obviously he found it difficult with me being there—his place was very small. Besides, I didn't want to stay there too long in case the police found me and charged Rob for harbouring me.

However, this last consideration set my imagination working: I devised a plan to get out of Australia, and persuaded Rob to play his part. I had recently met Aaron, an American marine who had sailed into Fremantle, and thought I had fallen in love with him. Aaron had now gone home, and I told Rob I wanted to get a ticket to Michigan so that I could join up with him again. I asked Rob to call the police and let them know that he had a girl staying with at his place who was an illegal immigrant from the USA. Aaron had given me a heap of information about his home town and I really believed this scheme was worth a try. Rob called the local police, told them my name was Sarah, and that I had stowed away on a Russian freighter from America, and jumped ship in Fremantle. The police asked Rob for my description, and Rob told them he was expecting me back at his flat in about fifteen minutes.

Sure enough, as I waited outside in the street, I saw two police officers arrive. Rob let them into the flat, and a few minutes later I knocked at the door. Rob let me in.

"Is this her?" one of the policemen asked. Rob nodded.

"Right-o, lovey, you're under arrest. We'd like you to accompany us back to the police station."

As we left I turned round and winked at Rob. *Nice one*, I thought.

The police took me into an interview room at headquarters. The hardest part of the charade for me was the American accent. I refused to answer most of their questions. The police searched my bag and found a few American items that Aaron had given me—some chewing gum, a pack of cigarettes, a few coins. They asked my age.

"Seventeen," I told them. (I was fourteen and a half.)

Sitting there in the East Perth Dock was a bit nerve-racking. I prayed to God that none of the police passing by would recognise me. At last a big, hunky detective walked in. "Well, Yankee gal, looks like we're sending you back to the States. We sure as hell don't want you here," he told me.

I looked up at him, pretending I was utterly dismayed by this news. "Oh, gee, please don't send me back!" I pleaded.

The police told me I would be interviewed by the Federal Police and the American Embassy to establish which ship I had stowed away on. I rattled off the name of a Russian freighter I knew was docked at Fremantle Harbour. After more investigation, the police were satisfied that I was telling the truth. I was told that my next port of call would be the Immigration Detention Centre. There, after a long wait, I was informed that I was booked on a flight out of Australia next morning. I assumed that I would stay at the Detention Centre that night, but the police then told me that because I was officially a juvenile, I would be taken to a place called Longmore.

Oh God, I thought, *I'm done for!* The police drove me out to

Bentley and I was placed in a cell at Longmore. Fortunately no one recognised me. Next morning, the police drove me back to headquarters. But suddenly I had second thoughts about this whole wild adventure. To be alone in America would be worse than being alone in Australia. "Look, I'm really Australian…" I said, lapsing into my own Aussie accent. They called Rob and he confirmed the truth of what I told them. The police then drove me back to his flat, and told us both never to try on anything like this again, otherwise we would both be arrested. So much for my flight of imagination.

Most of the street kids I knew in Perth seemed to get themselves banged—up-pregnant—or else locked up. There just didn't seem to be enough to motivate young people in the city. I was sick of it all, and decided I might as well return to Nyandi after all. This was quite a momentous decision. I hitch-hiked to the city from Rob's place and caught up with three other street kids I knew—Stix, who was sixteen, Ricky, who was only six, and Craig, the same age as me. They told me they needed money and were going to do a break-and enter and asked me to join them. Why not, I thought, it sounded like a bit of fun. Anything to break the monotony of that street life!

We stole a car and drove back to Nedlands, which we knew to be quite a wealthy suburb, and decided to break into a clothing shop. Stix, who was armed with an iron bar, told me to force open the back door, and we all got inside. I was freaking out: the shop was next to the hospital, which was patrolled by security guards. Stix said that if anyone came after us he'd give it to them with the iron bar. Ricky, young as he was, turned out to be quite a professional thief. I asked Stix for a light to search the drawers below the counter, and he told me to set one of the dresses on fire. So I did-and suddenly the whole dress rack burst into flames! I nearly shit myself, my heart pounded, and all I could think about was the fact that we were directly across the road from a service station. I imagined the whole street exploding.

The robbery was a complete waste of time: we scored only about ten dollars. We abandoned the stolen car and as we walked along the street I told the guys to start hitching, be cause the police would arrive any second. A green army truck took us about two miles along the road then dropped us off. It turned out that the soldier who was driving it had called the police on his mobile phone. The others were furious, but I felt relieved more than anything—I would get to see Robyn again, and be secure once more. That was important to me.

The police charged all of us except for Ricky, who was too young. I managed to see Lillian for a brief interview. She was not impressed by my behaviour, and gave me a lecture on my way of life. Although I had acted like a rebel, I was also a victim, deeply hurting inside. I think she understood that. At the court hearing which followed I was sentenced to a further six months in Nyandi.

nyandi again

⌘

The staff at Nyandi gave me a great welcome. They threw me into Time-out for three days, leaving me to count the tiles on the wall and watch the cockroaches running around. So it was back to the usual routine, including the hated behaviour sheets. After the first week I began to rebel. The staff really picked on me, and I slid into a deep depression. It was horrific; even talking to Robert, the psychologist, gave me no relief. I needed love, and I needed it now. I understood that the staff at Nyandi had a job to do; what I really rebelled against were the rules, the harsh punishment and the fact that we were all treated the same. We weren't the same, we were different sorts of kids with huge problems. No one ever tried to find out why I behaved the way I did: they simply followed all the rules. I realised that I got more attention when I behaved badly—I craved attention, but I didn't understand that I was only hurting myself. I began to cut myself again, every opportunity I got. I thought that if the staff saw me bleeding that would compel their attention. It did, but it wasn't the kind I wanted. I usually ended up being dragged back into isolation with my arms twisted behind me. The staff knew what I was doing, and decided the best way to deal with me was to ignore me.

The one thing I loved at Nyandi was school. There were two classrooms and we had a Chinese teacher, Janette, who was nice but strict. She didn't take any crap from the kids.

Unfortunately most of the other kids were quite uneducated, and that was hard for me, since Janette had to give most of her attention to them. I was frustrated by this, and played up a lot of the time in order to be noticed. One morning, another girl decided she was going to bash me up because she reckoned I'd taken her seat. I was really scared—I hated the thought of having my head kicked in. I decided to act. There was no glass available, so I quickly stuffed a small bottle of liquid paper down my bra, then kicked over the desk and shouted out to Janette: "You fuckin' Asian bitch!" I never meant it, secretly I quite liked her.

The alarm bell went off and the usual flock of male youth workers arrived. I really believe they enjoyed dragging us off to Time-out, that they felt a sense of justification and actually thought the punishment was good for us. Mitch grabbed me by the hair, twisted my arms and threw me into one of the solitary cells. As they locked the door on the outside tears streamed down my face. Every time I was punished like this I seemed to relive my mother's abuse of me. I got out the bottle of liquid paper and took a mouthful of it. Within two minutes I was choking—I couldn't breathe. I pushed the intercom button, and another youth worker, Sandra, came running. She could tell at once that I was really sick, and I was rushed to the Royal Perth Hospital, where I was put into intensive care with oxygen, drips and all the rest. The worst part was that I couldn't breathe because the liquid paper had temporarily destroyed the air sacs in my lungs. Being in intensive care was not a pleasant experience. I knew that the other people there, lying all around me, were fighting for their lives while I seemed hell-bent on trying to destroy mine.

I realised that somehow I had to change. If I continued this war of self-destruction I really would not survive. So when I got back to Nyandi this time I behaved myself. It was amazing the difference this made—even the staff did not seem so bad.

I completed my six months program and was told I was being sent to Watson Lodge again, in Northbridge. A staff member took me over to a block of self contained units attached to the main building. The unit was revolting, there were no concessions to comfort, just bare walls—it was like a gaol. I got really angry when I was told that I had to eat my evening meal there alone. All my life I had been alienated, segregated, isolated—it seemed never ending.

"Fuck you!" I shrieked, "can't you ever stop punishing me?"

The staff member told me to stop making a fuss and go inside—and I decided I would burn the rotten place down. I went and knocked on her door and asked for a some matches, but she refused to give me any. But a girl in another unit had overheard our exchange of words and she gave me a cigarette lighter.

I went back inside my unit. In return for all the pain I had ever felt I was determined to burn down that building. I set the mattress on fire; slowly the unit began to burn. I knew then I had gone too far—I had to get the hell out of there. I ran across the road and sat in the park opposite the building, hiding behind a tree. Soon the fire brigade arrived. As it turned out, there wasn't a great deal of damage, more smoke than fire.

Then the police came along and began to search for me; I stayed hidden beside the tree. Finally a station wagon drew up and Peter and Gordon, two of the Nyandi youth workers, jumped out. I knew they would drag me back to solitary confinement if they found me, but luckily they didn't. After the coast was clear I went to a phone box and called my policewoman friend, Aunty Lillian. She gave me a long lecture and told me to go back and try to behave. I knew she was right, but I also knew I would suffer. I was so sick of being punished.

Instead of going back I walked to my friend Rebecca's house—she was my best mate at Perth Modern High School. I asked if I could spend the night there. I knew her mum didn't really want me in the house, but she agreed in the end. Rebecca was lucky: she and her mum got along well, she had a great family. I really envied her. We spent most of the night playing the piano, which I loved. My sister Sofia used to have music lessons when she was a child and she was quite a good player. I kept nagging Rebecca to teach me to play my favourite passage from *The Moonlight Sonata*. We really had fun together. I cherished that time at Rebecca's house because it represented what I had always wanted. Next morning we woke early, and I decided that I would visit a local doctor to get a prescription for some pills. I knew Rebecca's mother wouldn't let me stay another night.

I found a phone box and searched the lists of medical practitioners. I was fifteen now, but I looked younger, and it was very hard to get a prescription. The doctors were always suspicious. Then I recalled a friend telling me that she'd been to this female doctor in one of the western suburbs who was well known for giving out drug prescriptions without too much fuss, so I decided to go there. I caught a bus and found the surgery. The doctor asked me what I wanted. I told her I couldn't relax, and ended up leaving her surgery with prescriptions for Valium, Normison and Temazepan, all relaxants. She told me to come back when I needed more. I was actually quite shocked at how easy it was for me to get the pills. But I walked out beaming from ear to ear. *God, this is fucking easy*, I thought. I caught the train back to Fremantle, where I hoped to contact Robyn. I really did miss her so much. I called her from a phone box down on the wharf, but she wasn't home, so I decided to try a few of the pills instead.

I entered a toilet block at Fremantle Wharf, where I met a girl called Cheryl, who told me she was a prostitute. As we talked I discovered she had experienced the same sort of life as me. She was twenty but looked ten years older, haggard and worn. But she was still able to laugh. She told me how much money she could make in one night, and how she used to rip off the American sailors when they came to Perth. I liked her style—I admired the way she told the world to fuck off, and didn't take anyone's crap. Cheryl told me she liked living on the streets because she felt free.

As she talked I had an idea. I asked her about the possibility of sailing off to America on one of the US warships. Cheryl told me she'd always wanted to do this but had never found anyone to share the exploit with her. Next morning an American aircraft carrier, the USN *Constellation*, was due to leave port: we both knew we could be on it. We found a lonely US marine from the *Constellation* walking along the Wharf and struck a deal with him. We planned to get aboard the ship posing as two marines, and he agreed to go back to the ship and fetch two uniforms for us. Dressed in these and armed with a couple of passes, we managed to get on board the aircraft carrier.

A marine called Roy took Cheryl and me into the marine berthing quarters. I jumped onto a bunk, pulled up a blanket and went to sleep, while Cheryl made friends with a couple of other young marines. Next morning I woke with a sudden jolt. The ship was under way—we were out at sea! Reality hit me. My God, I thought, *here I am on board ship with five thousand horny men!*

I got up and asked one of the marines to take me to the captain. I was scared and wanted out. Within minutes I was surrounded by military police, who handcuffed me and took me to the ship's hospital for questioning. It was decided that Cheryl and I would be flown back immediately to the naval base. Cheryl, too, had been having second thoughts about our adventure—I don't think she had enjoyed the previous night.

We had an excellent breakfast on board the ship and were then taken up to the flight deck where we boarded a helicopter which took us to the naval base. Here we were interrogated by the US Military Police and the Australian Naval Police.

I told them that my name was Samantha, and gave my age as twenty. Throughout the interview the Australian officer kept winking at me. The US Navy decided not to lay charges against us, and we were released straight away.

While Cheryl went off to work the streets, I telephoned a few hostels, but they were all full. I felt scared to be alone at night, and I began to cry. Although I liked to act tough, really I was still a little girl inside. I decided that if no one wanted me, than I would make them pay. I dialled Lifeline, and as I talked to a counsellor I began to swallow my pills one by one. The counsellor was nice and sounded caring, but I found it too difficult to tell her my innermost thoughts. Whenever anyone tried to come close to me I would push them away. I was so afraid of being hurt. Then the counsellor asked me if I was taking pills, and I told her I had swallowed a few. I said I was in a phone box near the Wharf. Soon everything went black and I passed out. Later, the police found me slumped near the water's edge.

I'd swallowed about eighty pills and woke up in Fremantle Hospital to hear someone saying: "It's her again" in an exasperated tone of voice. I had certainly succeeded in exasperating plenty of people—it seemed that the more I tried to make people care for me, the more I upset them. It was a vicious circle and I could see no way out of it. I was sick of overdosing myself and the nurses and doctors were extremely frustrated by my behaviour. In the end I told the hospital psychiatrist that if I was released I would kill myself. He didn't know whether I meant intentionally or as the accidental result of another overdose. He admitted me to the psychiatric ward. But being kept in hospital didn't really help me. I went through periods of deep depression. The doctors tried to make me talk about my problems, but I couldn't. I wouldn't. Instead, I'd sit in the garden and slash my arms. My emotions were frozen—they had been frozen ever since Allen, my mother's friend, had assaulted me all those years ago. I was cutting myself every day, and one morning a nurse caught me doing it. I begged her not to dob me in, but she said she had to. I must admit I was becoming a danger to myself, I just couldn't stop. The doctors told me I had to stop cutting myself. If I didn't, I would be sent to a detention centre (they had no idea I had run away from Nyandi) or a locked psychiatric centre (nor did they know I had been to Heathcote). After this I lost trust in the doctors, I thought they would send me to Heathcote, and I freaked out.

Outside in the courtyard I talked to Simon, another patient. He was about twenty, a heroin addict and suicidal: he had just slashed his wrist all the way up his arm. Simon told me he also wanted to get out of the hospital, but said that if we left together the police would come after us in force. We agreed to leave separately, and meet up at an address he gave me in Fremantle.

As I walked out of the hospital a nurse followed me and tried to stop me. "Please, Roxanne, we can help you—I know it's hard, but we do care about you!" she said. I was confused. Should I stop? Should I keep on going? I decided she was full of shit (I think that really I was scared to trust her) so I ran. I met up with Simon at his flat in the centre of Fremantle. He shared it with another guy who was also a heroin addict. Simon was hanging out, so he went into his bedroom and shot up. Within ten minutes he was as high as a kite—heroin obviously gave him what he needed and made him feel good. I, on the other hand, went into a bad depression. I only stayed at Simon's place a short while. I felt scared being around him and hated watching him destroy himself with heroin.

I telephoned Robyn again, and this time she was home. We arranged to meet up in Fremantle, at the bus stop outside Coles. I watched eagerly as each bus came along, and at last she arrived. We were so excited to see each other again! Robyn told me she was missing her sister, Katherine, who lived at

Collie, a small town about 100 kilometres from Perth. We had no money, so I suggested we take a cab and jump the driver. The poor cabbie seemed like a nice guy—he didn't deserve to be ripped off, and I felt guilty about that. When we drew near Collie, Robyn asked him to drive to the caravan park. "Okay here, girls?" he asked as he pulled up outside the entrance. The fare was over $100. I got out of the cab, telling the driver I would have to look for Robyn's father's van. As I ran off I heard Robyn bolt. The cabbie shouted for her to stop, and after a short chase he grabbed her and took her back to the car.

I had never been to Collie and had no idea where to go. After a while I decided to do the obvious thing and called the police station. The conversation went like this: "Hello, my name is Mrs Haysmith. Can you tell me if you have my daughter Robyn in custody?"—"Yes, we do. Would you like a word with her?"—"Yes, thank you, officer." Then Robyn came on the line. —"Robyn, it's me, Roxanne," I hissed. "I'm coming down to see you. I'll tell them I'm your sister Katherine, okay?"

I walked down to the police station. There was no sign of the taxi or the cab driver, so I figured he'd left. When I walked into the station the police officer on duty was as nice as pie. He really believed I was Robyn's sister and told me I could spend ten minutes with her. I had my pocket knife and some matches in my pocket, and I handed these to Robyn. We chatted on, then it was time for me to leave. As I walked to the front counter the cab driver walked in and I knew I was a goner.

"I see you caught the other one!" the cabbie bellowed.

"Which other one?" asked the cop. He looked at me. "This is her sister," he told the cabbie, who soon put him straight.

Well, all that former politeness towards me went right out of the window. The cop called me a little bitch and then threw me into the cell with Robyn. That did it. I knew I would be sent back to Nyandi, so I told Robyn I was going to set the police station on fire. I lit the mattress and within ten seconds the cell was billowing out thick black smoke. The police were beside themselves, and for one small second the fear went through me that they weren't going to let us out of there. But sure enough they came and we were handcuffed, thrown into a divvy van, driven to Perth Central Police Station and placed in the East Perth lock-up. I didn't really mind the police at East Perth. Most coppers would bash juveniles and push them around, but the East Perth cops were good. Robyn and I sat in the cells and waited for a van to take us back to Nyandi.

The chief thing that distressed me was the way I was always branded uncontrollable and suicidal. Even today, the police computers have "suicidal risk" after my name. When all the time all I ever wanted was to be loved.

Back at Nyandi, I was sent straight into Time-out. It always seemed such a waste of effort to me. Most of us at Nyandi were victims of child abuse, emotional abuse and rape, and sitting in Time-out only enhanced our pain. We would be led to a desk, told to face the wall, and weren't allowed to talk for days on end. The only way we could move from the desk was to go to the toilet: even that meant an extra fifteen minutes added to our punishment. One day I decided to rebel. I picked up my chair and threw it at the red iron door at the end of the dark, narrow passage. Lawrence, one of the youth workers, threw me into Cabin 11, the ultimate hell cell. I sat there and cried like a baby.

There was no toilet in cabin 11, just an iron bedframe. The only way I could hurt myself was to bang my head against the wall. I kept this up for an hour or so, until the pain became unbearable. Subsequently I ended up staying in Time-out for ten days. The law stated that no child should spend more than three days in solitary confinement. But the Nyandi staff knew how to get round that one: they would let me out after three days, then find an excuse to put me straight back again.

I cannot understand how, in 1983, the government of Western Australia could get away with so much abuse of the children in its care.

Eventually released from isolation, I was made to work in the kitchen, which I hated. There was a male chef who used to con all the girls for sex in exchange for cigarettes, luring them into the cool room or the storeroom. I couldn't believe that some of the staff were more untrustworthy than the inmates.

john: the journey begins

✏

This time, after completing my sentence at Nyandi, I decided to share a flat with a girl called Ellen. She was part-Aboriginal and very attractive. We got along well and managed to stay out of trouble. Our flat was in a high-rise block called Bay Apartments, right next to the Royal Perth Hospital. I was seventeen when we moved there.

Then, gradually, I found that it was becoming hard for me to make myself venture outside our flat, and after a few months I began to withdraw from the outside world completely. Then I suffered my first severe panic attack. It was horrifying. My whole body shook with fear, my heart raced and I blacked out. I didn't understand what was happening to me. I was also suffering another bad bout of depression. In the end I became completely housebound. I couldn't go out at all.

Ellen couldn't really understand it—all she knew was that I was too frightened to leave my room. I lived like this for months. Ellen and her boyfriend did all the shopping, and the only way I could keep going was by taking sleeping pills. It was weird. I would suddenly find myself quite unable to do the simplest task. I can only suppose that all the emotional trauma in my life had built up to a crisis. Ellen did as much as she could to help me, but she went out a lot of the time, and I was left alone.

I remembered that sometimes, in Nyandi, I'd had a fear of leaving the place, much as I loathed it, and I would deliberately ruin my program so that they would keep me locked up. I was very dependent on the system. Then Ellen went away for two days and I freaked out; all I did was lie on my bed, stiff with fear. In the end I called the shop in the apartment block and asked for some food to be delivered to the flat. The woman in the shop asked me to come down and get it. Although I was terribly hungry, I was too frightened to do as she asked. When I didn't appear, she called the hospital: within ten minutes a doctor and nurse were at the door of the flat. That was the kindest thing anyone ever did for me. The nurse was kind too, and the doctor held my hand as I cried—I was so scared. He gave me a Valium tablet, saying it would relax me. Then I was driven to the hospital next door.

The Valium knocked me out—I couldn't believe how stoned I was. In hospital I was put to bed and kept on medication for days. I wasn't properly aware of what was going on, all I could do was trust the hospital staff. After five days, the doctor told me that I'd had a panic attack and that I suffered from agoraphobia, a fear of open spaces. I thought it might as well be called a fear of fear. I was so scared all the time.

The doctors set up a desensitisation program, which showed me how to face my fear. I knew it was inside me; it did not lurk in streets or buildings. From the hospital I got in touch with Ellen's boyfriend, who was a street kid, and he and a few others came to visit me. But I felt so frightened and alone after they left. I also contacted Lillian, and she came with another detective to visit me. Then I decided to call John, the older man with whom Barry shared his flat. I hated the Valium they were giving me, and I asked him if he could bring me some sleeping pills instead. He came and brought fifty sleeping pills. He told me that he took them as well, and understood how I felt.

After this John and I became a lot closer. He was a complicated, sometimes devious character, certainly not your average bloke. He was also an alcoholic and turned out to be a very possessive man. But he was good to me at that time. He told me I needed a father and a decent home, and his words gave me enormous reassurance. I knew I had to succeed in beating my agoraphobia. Then he asked me if I would like to get a flat with him in Bayswater, another Perth suburb. I agreed, and he collected all my clothes from Bay Apartments, then came to see me at the hospital. He told me to sneak out of the hospital after he left and meet him in the street. I knew I had to act quickly: I was on a good behaviour bond, and it wouldn't take long for the nurses to contact the police and report me as missing.

John was waiting in his car and we drove to the new flat. It was great. He cooked my meals and took care of me. He even understood why I used to cut myself and never put me down because of this habit. About six weeks after we moved in together, he bought me a kitten. I called it Aisbett, after a journalist friend. I loved that kitten—he was my very own, my baby. I'd go to school occasionally and take him with me. But finally I gave up going to school, because most of the time I was still too scared to leave the flat. Gradually I was becoming completely dependent on John.

John had told me he was fifty-seven when I first met him at Barry's flat. I liked him immediately: somehow he reminded me of Ned Kelly. I recognised him as a rogue. But I discovered that he always had time to listen, and he never judged me—he just accepted me for what I was. There were, however, a few things about him I did not know. He was a convicted child molester and had a long criminal record. But so had I, so when I found that out it didn't bother me as much as it should have. After I moved in with John I started to make a few new friends. My closest friend was Tracey, who was only thirteen. We got along like sisters. John always liked me to meet new girls—I thought at the time it just showed he was a trendy guy, but I was wrong.

At Bayswater there were a lot of wild parties, ceaseless

noise and fights between neighbours. John decided to buy another gun for protection. The thought of having guns about the place made me feel safe. But because I was stoned most of the time, John used to hide the bullets. On my good days, John would take me out roo shooting. We never actually hit a kangaroo, but it was fun practising. He seemed great to me; I finally felt like I had found a dad.

It was about three months later that I started to notice the abusive side of John's nature. He would often watch me take a shower, but I was usually too scared or too stoned to worry about it. He was giving me about ten Valium a day—although I preferred other pills, I had simply got used to being drugged to the eyeballs with Valium. As a result, I spent most days in a blur. I know he raped me constantly, because I would often wake up and find my jeans around my ankles, or my clothing removed altogether.

One evening he asked me whether Tracey would like to sleep over at our place. When I invited her, she thought it was a great idea, because she was at loggerheads with her father at that time. John knew that Tracey's father didn't like him, and told Tracey not to tell her dad about it. That night, Tracey and I asked John if we could take a look at his gun, but he refused. We waited until he was asleep then picked it up and went out for a walk. I knew John would kill us if he found out. We decided to play a game and shoot out some soft-drink cans as targets. Then Tracey panicked and told me to bury the gun in case the police caught us with a loaded weapon. As it turned out, one of the neighbours had called the police after hearing gunshots. We bolted back to my place, where John asked us what we'd been up to. I told him we'd gone for a walk because we couldn't sleep, and then he asked us if we'd join him in a few beers. Tracey was a bit scared, but when she saw me drinking she gave it a go as well. I zonked out quickly. John had put three mattresses on the floor so that we could all be together, and I crawled into bed and flaked out.

It must have been around six in the morning when I woke to hear banging on the door. "Open up, Mr Darton!" an authoritative voice demanded. John told me to shut up and keep still. My head was hurting and I flaked out again...

"Come on, sweetheart, give me your arm." I wasn't sure if I was dreaming. I felt someone holding my arm and tried to sit up, but I was dizzy and my head still hurt. Then it all became clear. I wiped my eyes and saw that the room was full of police and ambulance drivers, and Tracey's dad was there.

Apparently her father had called the police because she'd run home after John tried to rape her. She told her dad that John had given her some pills then tried to assault her. She also said that John had hit me over the head. I was so confused that I couldn't remember a thing. John denied everything, and I chose to believe him rather than Tracey. Yet I knew she didn't mean to lie—she was so distressed, and at thirteen she was very naive and didn't even know what sex was all about.

But I knew John had done something by the way he was acting. He told me that it was Tracey who wanted to have sex with him and said he hadn't hit me, the damage to my head must have been an accident. The police wanted me to go to hospital and said they would interview Tracey later in the day. I was admitted to Middle Swan Hospital. I had concussion and my system was overloaded with drugs. They said it was too late to pump my stomach, but they wanted to keep me in for observation.

John arrived at the hospital and told me to discharge myself, saying he was the only bastard who cared about me, and that he wanted me to talk to Tracey to clear the air. I was terrified of losing John. He was the only one who understood me and my panic attacks; without him I felt I couldn't survive. I knew I needed him, so I got up and left the hospital. I walked to

Tracey's place and found her planked on her bed. Her dad had gone out, so I had time to talk to her. I told her to tell her dad that she had made it up about John, that it was all a mistake. If John was charged, I explained how he would have to go away, and I would go with him. I knew that Tracey didn't really like her dad, and finally she told me that she wanted to run away to her mum's place in Kalgoorlie. But I told her not to nick off, because she'd only get into trouble.

Tracey then told the police she'd made up her story, but they didn't believe her. Then they asked us if we'd been firing a gun the previous night. I told the cops I had used the gun, and told them I would give it to them so long as I wasn't charged. I didn't want to be taken away from John. I told them where the gun was, and when they found it I think they were shocked; they hadn't realised how powerful it was. And it was still loaded.

At the police station Freddy, a young constable, told me to put the weapon down and take out the bullets. Deep inside of me I didn't want to hand over the gun—I felt I was betraying John. Then the coppers charged me anyway for possession of a weapon, which didn't seem fair. I vowed never to give them anything or trust them ever again. I used John's surname so that Nyandi wouldn't find out I had been charged. I called myself Roxanne Darton. John came down to the police station and bailed me out. He didn't seem angry—I think he finally realised he had some sort of control over me, even if it was illegal. But that day, after we went home, it was clear that we were going to lose each other. By being found in possession of a gun and discharging a firearm, I had broken my good behaviour bond and when I went to court I knew the police would bring up all my old charges.

I called Lillian, and told her about the gun. I also told her about John, and my fear of going to gaol. She told me to stay where I was, and not to run away or hurt myself. Lillian was a great person, she was always there when I needed her. She was a wonderful policewoman who always gave me guidance and positive advice. I knew she was always right, but at this point I was too scared and I wasn't ready to listen to her or trust anyone. I told her I wouldn't hurt myself, and said I would call her again later.

John, Tracey and I met to talk. John did most of the talking. He wanted to go to Tasmania, his home state. Tracey said she wanted to go to Kalgoorlie and her mum. I didn't care where we went. In the end John decided we would drive off in the car and head for Kalgoorlie. We had no money, just my dole cheque and a bunch of stolen cheques from a robbery John had carried out. Tracey went home for her clothes and took some money. I took all my teddy bears, my school uniform and two pairs of jeans. As I left the flat I cried. I didn't really want to run away. But I had no choice: I was completely dependent on John, who was in charge of my medication and sleeping pills and knew when I needed them.

John's car was an old Holden Kingswood which had always got us from A to B, and I felt safe with John at the wheel. As we drove out of Perth the Valium made my head swim and tears flowed down my cheeks; somehow I knew that life would never be the same again. The radio played Michael Jackson's "Ben", and I wished my life had been different. I cried for the good life I never had and for the friends I was leaving behind.

I took out my razor blade and cut myself, and as the blood flowed out so did my sadness. John just kept driving, oblivious to what I was doing, drinking beer from a can. He realised the police knew our car quite well, and thought we should make for Kalgoorlie via Esperance and Albany. His main fear was that Tracey's dad would report her as a missing under-age person—and John was a convicted child molester.

After about three hours we decided to stop at Mandurah, a coastal town with wonderful beaches and lots of holiday makers. We pulled into a service station to fill up and John got me to pay with one of his stolen cheques. As I gave the cheque to the attendant my heart pounded with fear, my legs felt like jelly and I thought I would pass out. I ran back to the car and John told me I'd done well. It was nice to be praised. All my life people were always so quick to tell me about the negative things I was doing, but John never did that.

Tracey had fallen asleep, so John left the car to buy some fish and chips. "Don't be long!" I called. I got really scared when he went out of sight. I was so dependent on him, I needed him emotionally in order to survive. He brought the fish and chips and we ate them, then John took out a handful of pills. He gave me one and told me I could have the rest after I'd booked us in at a motel. "What motel—how come I have to do it?" I protested. "They'll never believe I'm over eighteen." It was true that at seventeen, I looked younger than my age. "Look, we need that room," John bellowed. "I'll drive up to the reception and you get out and do your thing. When you've finished, give me the sign." We managed to find the richest looking motel around and I went to reception and talked to the manager. I gave my name as Bethany. I booked a room, using another stolen cheque John gave me, and we all went inside. I never stopped to think how a motel owner would feel about being ripped off. At this stage I lived in a dream world most of the time.

John told me again that I'd done well, and gave me the rest of my pills. Tracey decided to take a shower and John went into the bathroom to give her the soap. It was hard for me to believe he was paedophile, like the police said—one minute he was a bastard, the next he was really nice. It seemed to me that John and I had the perfect relationship. He gave me pills and looked after me, and I stole for him and did whatever else he wanted.

We ordered room service, and after we'd eaten Tracey and I said we wanted to go to a fair we'd seen advertised. John gave me some extra pills because he knew I would start to panic and shake—he knew I still felt scared in the world outside. After taking the extra Valium I got very drowsy and John held my arm as we walked to the car. Tracey sat next to him and I lay down in the back seat. We drove for about two kilometres, then John suddenly yelled: "Roxanne, keep your fuckin' head down and don't say a fuckin' word, right!" The cop on our tail put on the blue light and John pulled over. "Where's the fuckin' rifle, Trace?" he asked.—"It's still under your seat," Tracey whispered.

The policeman asked John why his tail-light wasn't working. "Look, officer, I'll get it fixed at the next service station," John replied.—"Give us a look at your licence," the cop said. John sat there telling him a heap of lies, and said Tracey was his stepdaughter.—"Who's the girl in the back?" the cop asked. I was really stoned, my hair was matted and I was painfully thin.—"Oh, she's my daughter and she's retarded," John told him. I couldn't believe he'd said that. Then the policeman asked me my name. "Bethany," I told him. He turned back to John. "Okay, Mr Darton, you can go, but get that tail-light fixed."

John decided to give the fair a miss and drove back to the motel. He was angry that I'd spoken to the cop. "Next time let me do all the fuckin' talking," he said. "I know how to handle these pigs." At the motel he told me to go in and tell the man at the desk that we had to check out because we'd had news of a death in the family. The receptionist asked me how much we'd paid as a deposit and I said about $500. She gave me $300 and I bolted out of there. when I showed John the money he was really pleased, and I knew I had done the right thing once again. We found a Shell garage where John bought some supplies, extra fuel and drinks for the road. While he was in the shop this big dog jumped into the car, a huge German Shepherd. I begged John to let me keep it.—"Okay, keep the fuckin' dog, but if it shits you girls can clean up the mess," he said. It was great having Sheba with us. I called her Sheba because she sat up on the back seat like a queen.

We drove out of Mandurah quickly. John was getting more drunk by the hour. He figured we'd go to Kalgoorlie via Albany, then head down south. It took us three days to get to Albany. Most of the time I was shaking, so John used to stop the car at a roadhouse where we'd eat. The $300 from the Mandurah motel soon disappeared and we didn't have any more to book a room anywhere. It got cold sleeping in the car, and Tracey asked John if we could buy some extra clothes and a sleeping-bag.

"Okay," he said. "I'll give you girls another cheque. If anyone gets suss get the fuck outta there." He gave me the cheque and some pills. I was already really stoned, but he knew I got nervous being away from him and the Valium calmed me down. We both walked into a shop and we each bought three pairs of jeans and two blue jackets so that we'd look like sisters, even though my hair was pitch-black and Tracey was a golden blonde. She seemed older than her age, about sixteen, while I looked easily a year younger than her. We bought John a few shirts and some jeans as well, and got out of there quickly. Then we found a sports store and bought two sleeping-bags and a tent. That just about used up all the money.

Albany was such a beautiful town, and I asked John if we could have a look at the whaling station. He found a pub and spent the rest of our dollars on beer, then we drove to a park, where John told Tracey to find the toilets and return in ten minutes. When she was out of sight he grabbed the rifle and threatened me. "Look, Roxanne, I'm not taking any more of her crap. We're all gunna come undone because of that stupid little bitch. At Kalgoorlie she goes or else."

I couldn't believe the games he played. I wanted to talk to him but I knew it was no good, he was drunk and I was too scared. When Tracey came back I warned her not to do anything to upset him because he would take it out on me. He could see that I was starting to shake again and threw some pills at me. He drove us to a motel called The Dog Rock. It had a huge dog carved out of rock at the front and was quite famous. John made Sheba stay in the car. This time he decided not to pay by cheque because he didn't want to leave a trail of bounced cheques behind us for the police to discover. I told the receptionist that we would pay on departure and she accepted this.

As usual, John was starving. We ordered a huge lobster, prawns and steak. It was good to eat some decent food—most of the time we had hamburgers and chips and other junk, which I found hard to eat. After we'd eaten we went up to our room and I asked John if I could call Lillian, just to let her know I was okay. He slapped me across the face. "How can you be that stupid! We don't want the fuckin' pigs on our trail!" As I cried he went off in a huff to take a shower and then I took out the razor and began to cut myself.

Tracey decided to go out. John liked the idea but I didn't because I knew he would start touching me and trying to get me to have sex with him. Most of the time he could do whatever he wanted to me because I was too stoned to know what was happening. The times I was aware he was touching me I'd let him do it, because I was more afraid of losing him than anything. I think that even if he'd tried to shoot me I would still have stayed with him.

Now, after Tracey left, John ordered me into the shower. I refused at first, but he started to swear at me. I told him I needed medication and he threw me nine pills. Taking medication blacked out my remembered childhood pain as well as the pain I had with John. I had fallen into the habit of always taking showers with my clothes on because of the way he behaved. Now as soon as I got into the shower he started to touch me and I told him to stop. He went outside, swearing and I finished my shower. When he returned I heard him lock the door and saw he had the gun. As he pointed it at me I felt too numb to cry. He told me that I was his and he could do whatever he wanted with me. "I'm the only one who cares about you and knows how to look after you. If it wasn't for me you'd be in gaol, and don't forget it." He put me on the bed and I flaked out. It was true—he could do anything to me. I allowed it not because I wanted it but because I truly believed that he really did take care of me.

I woke up about four hours later. Tracey wasn't back. John had obviously had his fun with me because my shirt was completely undone. He sat on the bed and asked if I'd like a cup of coffee.

When Tracey came back she looked like she'd run a marathon. She said she'd seen a couple of cops and thought they'd recognised her. We knew that her description as a missing young person had been circulated. John told her to stick close to him all the time. He wasn't prepared to take the rap for her. He could be charged for harbouring a runaway.

We all stayed in the motel room that night—we figured it was safer to stay inside. We didn't want to risk being caught for the stolen cheques. John decided to get Tracey and me drunk, but I ended up flaking out from all the pills yet again. Next morning, Tracey told me John had tried it on with her again. I told her not to listen to him, but I knew he could become very aggressive and I could see that Tracey was really scared. She told me that when we got to Kalgoorlie she would stay there with her mum. Deep inside of me I didn't want her to go because that meant losing my only friend. I couldn't stand the thought of spending all day and all night without her and being alone with John. Yet it was very difficult for me to have any real contact with anyone else because I was so emotionally dependent on him. I couldn't be away from him for more than five minutes without feeling extreme fear and panic.

We got up early and had breakfast. Usually John only ate

once a day—something like sausages and bacon or an egg roll. He had a very unhealthy diet and so did I. I think my poor diet contributed to the fact that I was so lethargic most of the time. I rarely ate nutritional meals, and then only in small amounts. Drugs were far more important to me: I believed the only way to get well, to rid myself of depression and fear and panic attacks, was to swallow pills.

After we left Albany I sank into one of my deep depressions. I hated leaving Perth because I felt it was my home, and now I felt homeless. All my life I had been searching for security: when I left Perth I felt I was leaving the foundations I relied upon. As we travelled on from Albany to Esperance the weather was cold. We were sleeping in the car and living from hand to mouth. I spent most of the time sleeping and was too drowsy to comprehend very much at all. John drank as he drove, gabbling on to Tracey about how tough he was, and what a great drinker he was. He hadn't had much education and was very ocker—his life had always revolved around pubs and dubs. John always wanted to be in control, but that was what I liked about him. Although he wasn't frightening in appearance, he had a very aggressive streak and could become quite violent; yet at other times he was so caring. Although I hated his verbal and physical abuse, I still saw him as the man who could save me and make my life better.

Near Ravensthorpe we had almost run out of money and were without food or petrol. John decided that because I was the best talker, I should always be the one to act when we needed something. As we arrived at a country roadhouse, I went in and ordered three takeaway meals, while Tracey filled the petrol tank. I took the meals from the waitress and told her my purse was in the car. Calmly I walked to the car, slowly took out the gun, then walked back inside. "Give me everything in the till—notes only! Don't make me nervous or I'll shoot!" I told the waitress. She handed me twenty dollars, I fled back to the car and John hightailed it outta there.

Service-station robbery became a way of getting food when we were desperate. We knew the cops would be a fair way out of town, so we'd find a small creek or river and park there until John judged the coast was clear. Because our car guzzled so much petrol, we knew we'd be lucky to make it to Esperance. The petrol tank registered almost empty when John stopped at a farmhouse a few miles out of Esperance and ordered me to go in and beg for money. By now, after days in the car, I looked terrible and smelt even worse. 'John, I feel really sick, I don't want to do it," I pleaded.—"Look, Roxanne," he told me, 'just bloody get in there and stop stuffing around. Here's a tablet, it'll calm you down. Hurry up, we haven't got all day."

I took the Valium and knocked on the farmhouse door. There didn't seem to be anyone home, so I walked around the back. The back door was open and I walked in. I was petrified, but I wanted to make John feel pleased with me. As I searched the place I felt like someone was watching me, it was really scary. I found a cheque book, some cash and a string of pearls. I ran back to the car and we sped off.

"What did ya get the fuckin' pearls for, you stupid bitch?" John asked savagely.

"I liked them," I whispered.

"Fuckin' get rid of the bastards!" he retorted. He ripped them from my hand and threw them out of the window. The anger in his voice made me shake and I could sense the aggression about to erupt even before he slapped me across the face.

I decided to curl up in my sleeping-bag and hold on to one of my stuffed toys. I always found this comforting. Eyeing the petrol gauge, Tracey asked John how long it would be until we got to the next service station.

"Stop nagging, will ya, we'll get there when we get there," John snapped. We just made it to Esperance and John parked the car outside a pub. "Look, girls, I'm just going to get some beer. Don't move!" he bellowed. He bought two dozen cans of beer with one of the cheques I'd stolen.

John had a great driving record. He'd spent most of his life as a truckie and knew just about every road in Australia. We had a CB radio in the car, and John decided he would get it working so that he could find out where the coppers were. We also needed more Valium and sleeping pills for me. John would always get these for me. He'd drag me into a doctor's surgery and tell them all sorts of different lies. Either my mother had died, or I was his wife and had had a nervous breakdown. The most usual story, however, was that I was his retarded daughter and he was taking me to the next big town for treatment. He'd show the slash marks on my arms. The doctors always believed him and handed out prescriptions like lollies. John also got me to steal prescription pads, which he would fill in, then send me off to the chemist. He always rewarded me with some extra Valium after I got a prescription this way.

With another stolen cheque we got an aerial for the CB radio, food and petrol. Then John decided it was time to drive on to Norseman. It was very tiring sitting in the car for so long and we begged him to stop for a while. He just told us to shut up and look at the scenery. I was so sick and tired of travelling. I longed for a motel room and clean clothes. I'd worn the same clothes since we left Albany and I was filthy. John didn't like sleeping in the car and usually ordered Tracey and me to sleep in the bush alongside him.

I remember that particular night, after Tracey fell asleep, John told me he was horny and wanted me. I never wanted to love John in that way, but he kept harassing me and threw me roughly on the ground. I begged him to stop. Then he went to the boot of the car to get his gun. As I lay on the grass John pointed the barrel of the .22 calibre rifle at my head and told me he would shoot me if I didn't do what he wanted. He then unzipped his fly, urinated all over me, and raped me while I lay on the ground sobbing. I felt like killing him with the gun, but I was too scared to lose him. I knew Tracey would soon be with her mum and then John and I would be alone.

As we drew nearer to Kalgoorlie, Tracey was getting anxious about seeing her mother. She'd hated living with her dad, but was worried that her mum wouldn't want her. She knew she had found a new boyfriend. I told Tracey her mum would be happy to see her and things would be okay, and that seemed to calm her.

Norseman didn't seem much of a town as we drove into it— in fact I thought that if you blinked you might miss it. Maybe it was because my brain was so fogged up. John filled up with petrol, bought some food and told us we were going to camp for the night. It was too dangerous to go to a motel. We were still in Western Australia, and he knew the police could thrown me in prison if they found me. He had always warned me that if we got caught I should take the rap—that way he could bail me out.

We found a spot off the road and John pulled all the sleeping gear out of the car and set it up. The nights were really cold now and I began to feel very sick. I woke with terrible cramps in my stomach. John said it was because I wasn't eating properly, but I knew it was more than that. I begged him to take me to hospital, but he refused, until finally the pain became unbearable. Then he agreed to take me to a doctor. John was scared of losing me—l think he was just as dependent on me as I was on him. He got me to a surgery, where the doctor took one look at me, then told John I had pneumonia and was very rundown. He wanted to admit me to hospital immediately. John looked at me and I knew exactly what he was thinking. The doctor offered to drive me to the hospital, he was quite insistent, but John refused to let him do it. He said he would drive me there himself. He didn't; all he did was get me some Panadol.

John was nervous about the fact that he hadn't taken me to hospital and worried that the doctor would call the police, so we sped on to Kalgoorlie. It took me about two weeks to recover, but gradually I felt better.

From Norseman to Kalgoorlie I was in a total state of depression because I knew Tracey was about to leave us. She thought it would be good if we met her mother and stuck around for a day or two. When we arrived Tracey's mum wasn't at all what I'd expected. She was quite nice, but it seemed like she was caught up in her own life and not really interested in Tracey. She was very poor and lived in an old, rundown house which looked like a woolshed. When Tracey asked her if we could stay the night, her mum was really pissed off with the idea at first. Her boyfriend was coming over and obviously we'd be in the way. But Tracey finally got her mother to agree, and she asked if we wanted to go out for dinner with her and her boyfriend. She took us across the road to the pub and we all had a cheap, slap-up meal. I was really bored and still felt sick. All I wanted to do was sleep. I asked John to take me back to Tracey's mother's place but he wouldn't. I spent the evening listening to trucking and pub stories instead of being cared for in hospital, which I felt deep down was where I should be.

Tracey and I spent the rest of that night listening to the moans and groans that came from her mother's room. I managed to get about one hour's sleep. I told Tracey that her mum didn't really want John and me there, and I thought it would be best if we left. But we ended up staying there for three nights before John said it was time to move on. He disliked being in one place too long. At the pub he had cashed a cheque for $100. We filled up with petrol and drove non-stop back to Norseman because of that dud cheque. John was worried that the cops would have our descriptions from the pub.

across the nullarbor

❦

Just out of Norseman we started our trip across the Nullarbor Plain, heading towards South Australia. Driving through the countryside was really boring most of the time. John gave me enough pills to knock out a normal person for a week. I hated being stoned all the time, with everything a blur, but I didn't feel I was strong enough to cope with the world without Valium and John. Often as we were driving I would feel John's hands pressing between my legs. I hated this but I knew that if I put up a fight he would get aggressive or violent.

As we drove through the small country towns John would tell me stories about the Great Australian Bight and the Nullarbor, and about the lives of his truckie mates. His stories didn't really interest me—l just pretended to listen half the time, and went on dreaming about the new life I would have someday.

John needed to take a break from driving every now and then and he would pull over and tell me to get the rifle out of the boot. I remember him telling me that he would "kill any copper cunt who got in his way". I felt good when he said that; it seemed to prove to me that he really cared. Yes, there were some good times with John. I loved it when he bought me spray paint and I would paint pictures of Sheba on the outside of the car.

But most of that trip across the Nullarbor was a nightmare.

As we drove John became more and more drunk, as well as more abrupt and cranky. He wasn't a pleasant drunk—he would become dark, angry and violent. One afternoon I decided to talk on the CB radio and leave him to concentrate on the road.

"Does anybody copy?" I asked.

"Yes," came the voice of a truck driver.

"I've got a copy. What is your name?"

"Davo," he replied.

We started talking to each other. He asked me how old I was and where I was going. As we talked, John suddenly exploded and hit the brakes. "What are you doing, you fucking stupid bitch, you're mine and nobody else's!" He wrenched the CB radio from me and told me to open him another beer. He stayed in a rotten mood for the rest of the afternoon. I didn't really understand why he was so mad at me. I hadn't done anything wrong. I think he was just so possessive, and jealous of me even talking to another male.

As the hours of driving took their toll, I began to feel the sensations of a panic attack. I think what started it was the thought that I was so far from help if I did go into a full blown attack. I began to shake uncontrollably. "John, pull over!" I screamed as all the terrors and confusion of my childhood came flying into my mind. This is how it always happened: frightening and fearful thoughts and ideas would enter my mind and I'd immediately go into a panic attack, begin to hyperventilate, then black out. It was terrifying for me. For someone so young I was suffering so much. While most kids my age were at home and amongst friends, discovering the joys of life, I was addicted to drugs, living in a car and spending most days too scared to go outside. It wasn't much of a life.

John gave me a paper bag to breathe into, to stop the hyperventilation. He held my hand and told me to breathe slowly. After about ten minutes he gave me three Normison tablets, which always calmed me down. I hated having these attacks, they took away my independence and made me reliant on John for all my needs.

"One thing about the Nullarbor—you don't know how many dead bodies are lying out there," John said as we went on driving. He began to tell me gory stories of his life as a truckie. "I'd see so many young girls hitch-hiking," he said. "Half of 'em would end up raped or murdered. You're lucky I'm here to take care of you." I listened as he mumbled on between swigs of beer. John was my rock and I knew I had to keep him beside me, otherwise I wouldn't make it. I asked him if we could stop off at the next petrol station.

"Are you fuckin' crazy!" he responded. "The next one is full of Blacks—they'd sooner stab ya in the back than look at ya!" John hated Aborigines. I think he'd been bashed up by some Blacks in his younger days. At all events, he went to great lengths to avoid them. I told him that we'd have to stop, otherwise we'd run out of petrol. He didn't like the idea, but knew there was no alternative. Finally we arrived at a small petrol station at the back of an Aboriginal community. John told me to go in with a cheque—as usual, we had no cash.

"Sorry, luv, we don't take cheques, only cash," the owner told me.

"But we've run out of cash," I said, trying to persuade him to take the cheque.

"Like I just said, you hafta come up with the cash. I've been ripped off too many times and stopped taking cheques ages ago."

"Look," I begged, "we've got to get to South Australia, my aunty's very sick. Please help us."

But he just kept saying no. "The only way you're gonna get juice is to swap it for something. What've you got?" he asked.

I told him I would have to ask my dad. John told me to give him whatever he wanted. He just didn't want to hang around a place full of "Abos".

"What about a gun?" I suggested. John actually had three guns, one small hand-gun and two .22s. He told me to give the Aborigine the hand-gun. I walked back into the servo.

"What kind of a gun is it? Gimme a look," the Aborigine said.

I took him to the car boot and showed him the hand-gun. "Okay, luv, but juice is all ya get," he said. He ended up ripping us off, but John didn't care, all he wanted was to get out of there.

The Nullarbor lived up to its name. There were no trees; it was barren and cold. I knew we would have to start thinking about a destination, because John had promised he would get me some treatment for my panic attacks once we were settled. The thought of living in South Australia really appealed to me, but as a Taswegian John had different ideas. He told me we'd make a final decision after he had shown me the whole of Australia.

We finally made it to Maura and John thought we should camp there for the night. We took out our sleeping bags and John made me a nice cup of tea and a sandwich. I had recovered quite well from the panic attack. I climbed into the car and fell into a deep, relaxing sleep. Most of the time I would sleep only intermittently through the night, and often woke up shaking from fear. This time I awoke to the noise of banging on the car door.

"Hey, love, it's the police. Can you open the door?"

John was waking up in the front seat. 'John, John, the coppers are here," I whispered.

"What do they fuckin' want?" he yelled.

"Can you open the door, lovey?" the copper asked me again.

John nodded at me so I opened the door. "What's wrong?" I asked.

The copper burst out laughing and pointed to the car roof. "Is she yours?"

Sheba was sitting frozen up there—she'd climbed up and fallen asleep on top of the car. I couldn't help laughing too, it was the funniest thing I'd seen in ages. The policeman told me to get her down before bits started dropping off her. Then John came out and he burst out laughing as well. Slowly we managed to thaw Sheba out and then we got a hot cup of tea for ourselves. I always took three or four tablets each morning with a hot drink. This relaxed me.

John said we'd reach Adelaide in another four hours. He bought me a hamburger and we headed off again. Although our travelling was often a nightmare, at other times I liked the feeling that I was running away from my problems. I'd always been good at doing that. As we were out of cash, apart from three dollars given to us by a hitch-hiker we'd picked up, John told me it was time for me to go to work again. His notion of "work" was for me to break into houses and look for money or items we could hock, while he kept watch.

Two hours later we crossed the border. To me this felt like something to celebrate. I was excited we'd made it to South Australia. But there was no celebration, just John, Sheba and me in our old car. The thought that my life might go on like this forever continually haunted me.

Money was short. Apart from my unemployment benefit, around ninety dollars a week, we had nothing. And John would sometimes drink all we had in one day. Our only other source of income was thieving. Trying to convince John we didn't need to break into houses was like attempting to train Ned Kelly as a saint. John was someone who had been born without a conscience. The day we arrived in South Australia I told him it was getting too late to do any jobs. I hoped we might find an understanding priest who would help us out. But in the few larger towns we passed through all the churches seemed to be shut. John wanted to reach Ceduna before sunset. I knew he had ideas of knocking off a few houses before we reached Port

Pirie. Our car was so large it seemed to burn petrol faster than we could find the money to feed it.

"Look, Roxanne, you've gotta get money at Ceduna or we won't be going any further," he said at last. "And if we don't keep going the police will find us and lock you away, then you'll be up shit creek."

"I'm sick of robbing houses," I told him. "Let me find a priest and ask for help. Anyway, why do I always have to do the work?"

"You ungrateful little slut, I'm the only one you've got and you listen to me—or you'll be out there on your own."

There was no answer to that. My greatest fear had always been that I would be left alone and locked away.

We arrived at Ceduna about five o'clock. I asked John if I could go to the church to get some food. I promised him I would break into some houses after I had something to eat. We found a church, but the priest wasn't there. I saw a sign with his address and persuaded John to drive me to the house. As we drew up outside the presbytery I asked John for some pills but he said he wouldn't give them to me until I had broken into at least one house. I got out of the car; my legs were shaking and my hands were sweaty. As I walked up to the house I decided the best idea was to tell the truth. I knocked on the door and a middle-aged woman opened it. I guessed she was the house-keeper.

"Can I help you?" She stared at me with no concern or care in her expression.

"Can I see the priest, please? It's really important."

"He isn't here. Can I help you?" There was something about the woman I didn't like. I believe she thought I was a drug addict, and I resented her forming this idea without knowing anything about me and what I was going through. I poured out my story, telling her that we had no money or petrol, that I suffered from agoraphobia and a panic disorder, and that I was hungry and tired.

"I can't believe you're agoraphobic if you were able to travel from Perth to Ceduna," she said, staring at me.

"Look, I'm on medication, I'm okay when I'm medicated," I told her desperately.

She sighed. "Well, lovey, I know your type. The best I can do is make you a sandwich—do you want Vegemite or cheese?"

"Cheese, please," I answered as she shut the door, making me wait outside like a dog expecting its supper. I felt humiliated, but what could I do? I really was starving.

I returned to the car and showed John the sandwiches. He didn't have to say anything, his face showed me his reaction: "I told you so".

We then drove around a few streets while he sussed out the houses. He stopped outside one house which seemed ideal to him. He was pretty sure no one was at home.

"John, I'm not going in, it's too risky. The people could come back at any moment. Please let's wait until tomorrow," I begged.

"We're not fuckin' waiting till tomorrow, go in now or you'll have to wait a long time for your pills."

"Okay," I cried, "I'll go in, but please keep watch. I'm just so fucking *scared*." My legs felt like jelly. I was always frightened there might be someone inside with a shotgun, waiting for me.

I knocked on the front door and waited. There was no answer so I walked around to the back. If someone saw me I would just say I wanted to ask for directions. As it turned out there was no one home. I ran back to the car and told John. I wanted to make sure he was protecting me, not just drinking. He pulled my head through the window and showed me the shotgun. "Well, go and smash a fuckin' window then, but hurry up."

The windows were pretty high; the only way to get in was to smash one. I picked up a rock and hurled it through the glass. As I climbed in I felt blood trickle down my arm and wrist. I found a bag and a cheque book, then opened the front door and ran to the car. My heart was beating a million to one. I didn't realise how badly I had cut myself climbing through the window. I told John the cut needed stitches.

"Are you kidding me!" he screamed. "This is a small fuckin' town, people talk-I'll buy you a bandage." He found a chemist and bought a small bandage which was covered in blood after a few minutes. I ripped up my school dress to make a proper bandage. I knew I would have to get the cut seen to and couldn't wait until we reached Adelaide. Mean while I looked through the bag and found $300 in a purse.

"You beauty!" John yelled out, smiling. Once again I had pleased him and I felt good. After that John was in a great mood all the way and promised he would take me out for the evening when we arrived in Adelaide.

Driving from Perth had taken its toll on me. Somewhere beyond Kyancutta, a small wheatbelt town, I had a major panic attack. I hyperventilated myself into a fit. I begged John to stop, but he kept driving. Then; as he looked at me, he knew it was serious, so he pulled into a farming property. I remember a woman calling an ambulance, then being driven to Kimba Base Hospital. When I arrived the doctor and the hospital staff realised I was thoroughly rundown and were very caring towards me. I had stomach cramps and they asked if I was pregnant. In the back of my mind I knew this was possible because John was always touching me; most of the time I was so drugged that he could have done anything to me. He was beside my bed and when he heard the question he became really offensive and threatened the staff.

John said he would park right outside the hospital and stay there until I was released. Later he came into my room and ordered me to discharge myself. I begged him to let me stay there for just one day—I was scared I might have another attack. He knew this could happen, so he agreed. The hospital staff gave me a shower, stitched my arm and I began to feel human once more. Next morning, John was there again, arguing with the staff about visiting me. He told them he would blow their brains out if he couldn't stay with me. I ended up discharging myself to avoid a confrontation.

After this we drove non-stop till we hit Adelaide. I was asleep from all the pills he'd given me when he shook me awake. "Have a look at the lights, Roxanne," he said. "We're in Adelaide."

adelaide

❧

We pulled over and parked and we both slept through until next morning, when a drunk woke us up, knocking on the window. "Hey, ya can't camp 'ere, the coppers will 'ave ya," he told us. John recognised his tune and invited him to breakfast. He wasn't very good company, that old dero. He stank to high heaven and was dribbling all over the place. But john had a good time. We found a hotel where we sat down for a decent breakfast and the two of them started talking about all the pubs they'd ever been to. John had a beer with his breakfast—he always started the day with a pint. I didn't understand how he could drink beer so early, but I couldn't really talk—after all, I was taking Valium all day every day and my brain was in a permanent fog.

After we got rid of Wilbur, the dero, John took me on a tour of Adelaide. It was a beautiful city, so clean, and part of me yearned to stay there. He found the casino, built in the old Victorian railway station, and told me he would take me there. We tasted "floaters" from the famous pie carts—meat pies and peas floating in gravy—and drove around the city for five hours.

Then I asked John about my medical treatment, and he took me to a medical centre. We sat in casualty and a doctor came out and talked to me. I explained about my agoraphobia and panic attacks, and a bit about my life. He seemed very interested in helping me and went off to see if he could admit me to hospital. John went after him—to support my need for treatment, he said. When they both finally reappeared, the doctor told me there was no bed available, and advised me to try for admittance to a hospital in Sydney. Apparently John had told him that was our next destination. I couldn't believe it— the doctor had seemed so nice, then he had suddenly switched right off. I felt totally pissed off and as we left I burst into tears. I told John I hated all doctors and would never ask for their help again. Later I learned the truth: apparently John had told the doctor I didn't really need treatment and shouldn't be admitted. I was really angry about this. I don't know why he did it. All I could think was that he was afraid to lose me. I made up my mind to get off the Valium and recover, then I could escape from John. Someday...

He could be such a bastard sometimes. But shouting at John never achieved anything—he would end up winning by yelling at me and insulting me. So I held it all in, and tried to deal with my anger by taking more pills to block it out.

John realised I was feeling low and remembered that he'd promised to take me out. He did. He took me to the Crazy Horse strip show and blew all our money on enjoying himself. It was a revolting evening: he spent most of the night offering me to the club manager as a stripper. He told him I would work all hours. I didn't want to join the strippers, but John didn't care. He never asked me how I felt, he just told me: "Roxanne, I've got you a job. You'll start tomorrow, it's easy work and good money."

For the first time in ages I exploded. "I'm not gunna work as a stripper! I hate you, how could you bring me to a strip club? I hate you!"

He grabbed me by the arm and pulled me aside. "I'm telling ya, you're gunna bloody work, it's for both of us, it's either this or the streets. If you don't do it I'll blow ya fuckin' head off."

There was no way I was going to work as a stripper—I'd rather die. So I took the second option he'd offered me. I'd ripped off men before, it was easy, and if I had to do something I'd rather go on the streets than have two hundred filthy eyes perving on me. We left the club early. I'd had a horrible time and so had John. I knew he was really pissed off with me for ruining his night out. He dragged me roughly to the car.

"Okay, John, I'll work for us, but I'm not stripping. I'll work the street and rip off, but only if you keep watch over me."

I stood outside a shop looking like a cheap hooker. It was degrading, standing there watching all the well-dressed women walk past, staring at me like I was the scum of the earth. Young men who came by would sneer: "How much for a root?" I knew I was there under false pretences, but it was real enough to feel the pain the other professional girls must experience. I stood there for an hour. I could see John parked across the road, waiting for someone to pick me up. He'd told me to take them around the corner to the car park to make some money and he was serious.

A few guys walked up but they wanted me to go for a drive with them and I refused. I'd never get into a car, it was too dangerous. Then this well-dressed young guy approached me. "Hi," he said, "you're a pretty girl—working, are you?" Surely it was obvious, I thought. "Yes," I said, "let's go if you want to." As we walked around the corner I could sense John watching me. We sat down on a bench and the young man introduced himself as Cyril. He was about thirty, not particularly good-looking. *God*, I thought, *what do I do now*? Then he said: "Look, love, I'm not like all the other other guys, I'm a born-again Christian," He poured out his story and in exchange I poured out mine. I couldn't believe it. The first job I'd got, and the bloke wanted to convert me!

"Lovey, I always come here on a Friday night to talk to the girls, because God has a better plan for each one of you," he said.

"Look, Cyril," I told him, "if I don't make some money tonight I'm in deep trouble." I told him about John and why I was doing this.

"Here's fifty dollars, it's all I can spare, but I hope it helps." He gave me his card as well. I was in slight shock. I ran to the car and told John all about it. "You beauty, I knew you could do it," he said. "A couple more and we're right."

I couldn't get over Cyril. Most girls pick up a proper job and have to go through with the whole thing. I got Cyril. I tried to think about all the things he'd told me, but I was too stoned. John had given me five more Valium, and I was getting drowsy.

Standing there in Hindley Street wasn't my idea of fun—there were heaps of weirdos walking past me. I couldn't believe it when two young coppers came up to me and started asking me the prices. "I'm not working," I told them, "I'm waiting for a friend." They smiled and walked off. At that point John came over towards me, and looking over, I saw a young guy peering into his car. John saw the guy and went back to ask him what he was doing.

"Police!" he shouted. "I'm going to search your vehicle for marijuana."

He started going through our possessions, and when I asked to see his badge he ran off. John was fuming and so was I. He pulled out the shotgun and gave it to me, then started the car. "When you see him I want you to stop him," he told me. "Okay?" We drove to an alleyway where I saw the guy and showed him the gun. He panicked and managed to get away, but a few people had seen the gun. John and I went back and parked in Hindley Street, and he told me to get out of the car again.

I walked back towards the place where I'd stood before, then I saw two policemen walking towards the car, so I ran back and jumped in. I grabbed my razor blade and the last two Valium pills I had and waited for the coppers to question us.

They told John that someone had seen the gun poking out of the car window, and warned him he might be arrested. Then they stripped the car apart and called a backup police car, and I knew we were goners. I begged the police not to take John away from me. He told them I was sixteen and mentally retarded, and so they took me too.

At police headquarters John was taken upstairs for questioning. I was kept at the front counter and basically treated well. I wasn't locked up. A policeman gave me some paper and a pen to occupy myself. "I want my dad!" I screamed. A policewoman told me everything would be okay, he was being talked to and they would have to keep him there to find out more about him. Then they told me that I would have to go to SARAC, the South Australia Remand and Assessment Centre, to be looked after. I knew exactly what they meant. I asked the police where they had put our car, because I wanted to see Sheba, my dog. I was as high as a kite because I'd swallowed my last pills in the police car.

I knew I had to get out of the police station to reach the car. I was petrified of being without John—I knew I couldn't survive. The only option was to break him out before the police found out his real identity and mine. I was sitting behind the front counter, right beside the double entrance doors. I had a spare set of car keys and when a man walked in to report a stolen motorbike, my moment arrived. There were only two police on duty there and as one of them took the details of the motorbike, the other officer went out the back. I jumped the counter and ran off through the doors as fast as I could into the police station carpark. I heard the copper behind the counter shout at me as he set off in pursuit and I managed to dive under a parked car. The policeman ran past me, calling my name.

I waited for ten minutes until I was sure the coast was clear, then looked around for the vehicle impounding section and managed to locate our car. By now it was pitch black. I started up the car, reversed out of the carpark and took off at high speed. I heard the police screaming out at me to stop, but it was too late. I didn't have the headlights switched on and crashed into an alleyway. I was lucky to escape with only a few bruises. I sat there dead quiet so that the cops wouldn't see me. Then, about five minutes later, I heard the police talking to Sheba: "Go, find her." You wouldn't believe it, Sheba led the police straight to our car!

I lay inside really still, hoping they wouldn't see me, but they shone their torches straight at me. "Is she okay?" I heard one of them ask. I burst into tears then, because I had failed and I knew my fate.

Back at the police station they were pretty nice to me. I wasn't sure why, but I figured they must be worried about me. A policewoman came in and started talking to me about John. "We have his record, darling—are you his daughter or stepdaughter? Where is your mother?" I told them John was my stepdad and that my mother was either in Melbourne or Tasmania. I said he was the only one who cared about me. He had told them I was his stepdaughter and had given my age as sixteen.

Then the policewoman said that she knew John was molesting me. His record showed he had been convicted of molesting two other children. I knew he was like that, but I did not really want to believe it. The policewoman asked me more questions, and told me John would be charged with having an offensive weapon, and that other charges were pending. She tried to convince me to have him charged with molesting me, but I refused to answer her questions. Then the police took me to the remand centre.

I knew there was only one way out, and that was to slash myself, which I did as soon as I arrived. After this I heard one of the welfare workers telling someone on the phone that they couldn't cope with me, and as I hadn't been charged or convicted they were going to send me to a hostel. The police arrived and I was driven to the hostel, somewhere in Adelaide.

It was an old building and Alice, the worker there, was old as well. For the first time in ages I was in a real bed, but I was too stressed to sleep much. Alice woke me in the morning. I knew I had to get to John. She said I wasn't allowed out, so I told her I would smash the place apart if she didn't give me my property and let me go. Deep inside I felt bad about this—I could tell that she was distressed at my threats. She gave me all my property and I caught a cab to the courthouse. John was called up and was granted bail with self-surety. If he failed to turn up later for his court appearance he would forfeit $500. I was so relieved to find him again, even though it was only about twenty-four hours since we had last seen each other. I was a nervous wreck from being separated from him.

John gave me a hug and told me they would never take me away again. "The next time they try I'll fuckin' blow 'em away," he said. He asked me about the questions the cops had put to me and I told him everything—I was totally faithful to John. He was pissed off that the police had interrogated me; I think he felt he was the only one allowed to have control over me. I had always given away my power, I had no control, and I felt safe that way.

He told me it was time to move on, that the cops would be on our tail. He gave me some pills, because by now I was shaking, and we headed out of Adelaide. Neither of us had any money left and I knew we wouldn't get far.

He echoed my thought. "We're going to have to do something or we'll be stuck in this cunt of a city," he said.

"Look, John, can't we go to the Welfare people—I'll go if you come with me."

"*No*," he snapped. He was still pissed off with being held in the cells for so long, and his alcohol withdrawal didn't help matters. "No," he repeated, "we'll get ourselves a hitch hiker."

"Oh John, I don't want to do that—why don't we just ask them to help us out instead of—you know..."

John would pick up young hitch-hikers and threaten to dump them off in the middle of nowhere if they didn't pay up. I thought that was pretty mean, but since I knew the alternatives I always did what he wanted. My ultimate fear was being left alone. I would have held up banks, done anything to avoid it. All my life, in the various institutions where I had lived, I had been left alone for hours at a time. For me, John represented normality.

Being on the road once again was hard. Sometimes John would get so mad he wouldn't even let me go to the toilet alone, he would make me hang on or else pull up in the bush and watch me. He was so scared of losing me. And he became so jealous when other people looked at me, especially other men.

After leaving Adelaide we picked up a young Swedish backpacker. He would have been in his early twenties. He sat in the front seat to begin with, then John ordered him into the back. As we drove John told him all about his guns, and I could sense the young Swede beginning to get really nervous. He asked John to let him out at the next town, but we kept on going. As John speeded up, a police car pulled us over and the Swedish guy got out.

"That was all your fuckin' fault," John said to me.

"What did I do?" I protested.

"You're supposed to be fuckin' agreeing with me. Liked him, did ya?" John's jealous streak was shining through and I waited for him to explode. He ordered me to lie down, and a policewoman came up and asked him to do a breathalyser test. The young backpacker took off pretty quickly. I was relieved to see him go; he was too nice to rob.

The police let us go after John passed the test. For once he was beer-free—and I could tell he wasn't enjoying it. "I've got fuckin' desert mouth, Roxanne," he said as we drove on. "I need a beer. We're gunna stop at the next town and ya gunna get me some money."

"I don't want to. Why don't you do it for a change? You always get me to do things I don't want to."

John was totally stunned by this. "Getting smart, are you?" he shouted. He pulled up at the next phone box we came to. "Go on, fuck off, you little bitch." He threw twenty cents at me and told me to call someone.

I knew I'd said the wrong thing and burst into tears. "Please, John, don't leave me. I'm sorry. I need you, don't leave me. I'll do anything, okay?"

"No one wants ya, ya stupid bitch. I would've found ya and shot ya if I'd caught ya with anyone else, anyway."

At this I climbed into the car, he gave me a few sleeping pills and I flaked out.

It was pitch-black when I woke. John had pulled up and had one hand on my breast. I pulled away and he told me yet again that I was his, that he owned me. Most of the things John wanted me to do were horrific. I had given him total control of my life and sometimes of my body as well. There were so many times when I cried myself to sleep. I felt as though my life was a big void, like I was living in hell. I was so unhappy. Every day I prayed I would find someone who would love me, not for my body or to persuade me to do bad things, but with a love like a mother's. I longed to be held. Sometimes I lay in the back seat of the car holding my teddy bears, just hoping that one day I would be really loved. I remember having this dream even when I was seven. It seemed such a simple desire, but the more I searched for love, the more elusive it became. I had begun to think that things would go on the way they were forever. I often thought about Lillian and the friends I had left behind. At times part of me even wanted to be back at Nyandi—at least I would have been closer to my mother.

We camped that night on a dirt track. As soon as I awoke in the morning John stuffed Valium down my throat. Whenever he bribed me with pills I knew he wanted me to do something. He drove around town looking for the right house to break into, and I knew that as usual, I was the one who would do all the work. He bought me a cup of coffee; this, combined with nineteen Valium pills, made me feel absolutely stoned. I wasn't afraid of anything now, I was just like a zombie.

We pulled up outside a house surrounded by a high brick wall. There was a dog, a bull terrier, which scared me. John told me to give him some meat from the hamburger he was eating. The dog took it and I bolted over the fence at a thousand k's an hour. All the doors were locked but I knew I had to get in, otherwise I would never hear the end of it. John had given me a jemmy, but I couldn't work out how to use it, so I picked up a rock from the garden and hurled it through a window. I felt pretty guilty, but I was desperate. I climbed in the window and looked through the house. It's really strange breaking into someone's home. You feel like you're intruding and you never know who might live there, or whether they might suddenly turn up. I hated this house because it was so nice. The kids' rooms made me feel sick. I was so jealous and deliberately messed them up and threw things around. I was pissed off that all this was theirs and not mine. I managed to get a tape recorder, a few dollars and some jewellery. John always told me to get things we could sell. He didn't want anything that could be traced. Before we left that town we sold the jewellery to some street kids and flogged the stereo at a shop. Breaking into the house didn't really seem worth the risk.

I was so tired I spent most of that day in a drug-induced sleep, clutching my teddy bears. When I woke I asked John where we were going. We were just driving around the countryside; we were still quite near Adelaide.

"I dunno," was his reply. He never really told me what was happening.

Then I started to think about getting off the pills, and the things Cyril had said kept flashing through my mind. "John, I want to get better," I said. "Will you take me to a detox centre—can we go back to live in Adelaide? I don't want to keep going. I'm tired and sick."

'The best bloody hospitals are in Sydney," he replied. "I'll get ya fixed up there. Trust me. I know what's best. I'm telling ya, Sydney's the go. We'll set offfor New South Wales soon."

I decided to believe him and hang in there until we got to Sydney, where he said he would get me admitted to the Royal North Shore Hospital.

Travelling and being on the run brought terrible stresses and strains. I hated having to worry about the police all the time and never having enough to eat. I was really living off pills—John would shove them down my throat faster than I could swallow them. My hair was filthy and matted and I refused to have showers because I was petrified that John would come in and touch me. My weight was down to forty two kilos, way too little for my height. But I didn't realise all this at the time, because I had placed my life so blindly in John's hands. Many nights he would threaten me and make me have sex with him. He always told me he was the only one I had in my life who cared about me. In some ways this was true, but he also used to abuse me cruelly. I decided this strange, incestuous father/daughter relationship was all worth it. It was a fantasy, but my whole life was so unreal that it was hard for me to tell when reality ended and fantasy began.

We went on driving through small country towns and things were always the same. John would get me to break into houses or accompany him to doctors' surgeries. I told him I didn't want to keep on doing these things because sooner or later I'd get caught and I didn't want to be separated from him. He exploded and told me there would be no more Valium if I didn't behave.

One time, just out of Adelaide, he made me tell a doctor a long sob story in order to get another prescription. Afterwards he drove to a carpark two minutes from the chemist's shop and ordered me to go in.

I began to cry. "I don't want to, can't you see I'm shaking?"

He told me he would leave me. "I don't care!" I cried out. "I want to go home, I'll leave, I can't take this any more! If you want to go, I don't care."

He slapped me across the face, drove off to a dirt track and tied my hands together in case I tried to run away. Then we drove back to the carpark, where he went off to the chemist's himself. "If you try to run you'll go down with me," he said. I knew what he meant. There was no escape. I was too scared to run because I couldn't handle my life on my own. I was terrified of having a panic attack, so I stayed. Sitting there in the carpark I saw a woman get out of her car. She was an escape route, but I was too scared and too embarrassed to do anything about it. I just sat and cried and waited for John to return.

When he got back he said he would release my hands if I behaved. He knew he had me under control again emotionally. He took the ropes off and gave me some Valium. I was in a terrible state and he calmed me down. "I love you, Roxanne, you know that," he told me. I wondered why he had this pattern of hurting me, then telling me he loved me. In the end I just accepted his abuse because I knew I had no option. Otherwise I would lose the only stable thing in my life. My whole life depended on him.

As we approached Adelaide again, I asked John if I could call Lillian. I really needed someone to talk to, and Lillian was one of the few people who had never used or abused me. She always made sense. John hated Lillian because of her job, because she represented power. He was always aggressive about the police. He told me I wasn't to call her because she would try to get us arrested.

"I won't tell her where we are," I pleaded, and finally he relented and we pulled up beside a phone box. John stood right outside so that he could hear what I was saying.

"Roxanne, you've got to come back. Where are you? Are you okay?" Lillian asked. I really couldn't say what I wanted to, part of me was asking for help, but I just couldn't tell her what had been happening. She would have told me to catch a bus back to Perth, but I knew I couldn't have lasted that vast empty distance by myself because of my agoraphobia. I was stuck. As I said goodbye I began to cry. I knew it would be a long time till I saw Lillian again.

"Are ya happy now?" John grunted as I climbed into the back seat. He ordered me into the front and said: "I know it's been a bit rough, Roxanne. Why don't we go and get a hotel room?"

We still had a few cheques from the last house I'd broken into, so we drove around the city and chose a posh-looking hotel. I was glad we'd come back to Adelaide; I liked it here. I also knew we could still turn around and go back to Perth. But there was no way John would go back there, and he was determined to keep me with him at all costs.

He wrote out a cheque and sent me into the hotel, telling me to book a room for five nights. The receptionist was extremely helpful and showed us to our room. It really was a beautiful hotel. The room had two single beds, so I knew I would be safe for at least one night. John ordered his usual case of beer and made me order the food. He would never let me eat in a motel restaurant; we always sat in the room. The Valium had taken away most of my appetite, but the food looked good. After dinner I settled down to some homework. I was supposed to be doing my Higher School Certificate by correspondence. I used to send off my work every three weeks, and my results were sent to city post offices where I would pick them up. John sat there watching me, brooding. Even though I'd known him for almost two years, I still didn't know much about him. He kept many dark secrets, especially about his criminal past. All I knew was that he had been married for a while. I guess I felt safer not knowing any more. But I knew there was something in his past that stirred him to deep anger.

Presently he told me it was time for me to take a shower. He knew I was terrified of this, and he enjoyed it. I said I was really tired, I would have a shower in the morning, and he gave me some sleeping pills before I crawled into bed. As I closed my eyes I could hear him slurping his beer and talking to himself. In spite of the pills I didn't get much sleep: the fear of what was to come kept me awake and anxious. I feared everything. Especially a shower.

In the morning John woke me early and told me to order breakfast. "And now I want you to get in that shower—you stink!" he screamed at me. "And you can wash these." He threw his socks at me. I decided there was no way out of it, but I was petrified because he pointed his gun at me. I still always showered with my clothes on. As I turned on the water my legs gave way and I began to faint. John carried me to the bed dripping wet and when I came round he said I must have fainted because I hadn't been eating properly. Then our breakfast arrived and he made me eat every scrap. I felt sick but I knew I probably needed it.

We stayed in the room for most of the morning. John was becoming paranoid that the police would catch up with us. Finally he said we couldn't hang around any longer, it was time to move on. Slowly he took all our gear and put it in the car boot. Then he told me that Sheba was becoming a pest and we had to get rid of her.

"Please don't kill her," I begged.

"I'm not a fuckin' bastard, you know," he replied. But I wasn't so sure. When we were living in Perth he had killed my cat, Aisbett, because he was jealous of the attention I gave it.

"We'll let the dog go in a field or out bush," he said.

I knew John hated Sheba shitting all over the place, and I could see his point of view. It was also difficult having the dog with us because we couldn't take her into motel rooms, and whenever we had to lock her in the car she would start to howl.

John sent me to reception to check out. The receptionist was surprised. "You haven't stayed long," he said.

"Well, we've had word that my uncle has died suddenly and we have to go to the funeral. I'm disappointed we can't stay any longer. Look, my dad paid for five nights in advance, so could you work out the bill?"

The receptionist gave me $300 change from the cheque I'd handed over and wished me luck. I hadn't really expected to get so much. When I showed John the money he was over the moon. He spent most of it on drink.

I was depressed by the fact that we were about to leave Adelaide, and that I was to lose Sheba. Now I would have no one but John. I felt alone inside. Occasionally I would think about the friends I'd had at Nyandi. I wondered how they were. I was getting further and further away from them. Many times I thought about taking an overdose to ease my pain, but I knew that John would never give me all the pills I would need. Cutting myself seemed the only way to ease my emotional pain. John never minded—he told me I could go on doing it so long as I didn't get blood on my clothes.

We drove through some country towns outside Adelaide, and along the way John kept looking out for a place to lose Sheba. I had wanted to leave her at the dog pound in the city, but John refused to go there. We ended up leaving her near a farm about fifty kilometres beyond Adelaide. I cried my eyes out. John didn't seem to care, he just went on drinking his beer, making me open can after can. We drove non-stop until we reached the New South Wales border at Mildura, a beautiful wheatbelt town. John thought it would be an experience for me to camp on the Murrumbidgee river bank, so we found a place to park and he set up the sleeping bags.

That night I learned a little more about John when I asked him if we could get someone else to share our journey. "I miss all my friends," I told him. "I'm sure there would be other kids who would love to join us." I was talking about finding a street kid like Tracey for company.

"If you want a kid you'll have to help me," John said.

"Help you do what?" I asked.

"Take one," he said. "How about a baby—would you like one?" It sounded as though he was planning a kidnapping.

"No, John, I don't mean that, I don't want to kidnap a baby, I want a friend," I said.

"But I'd love a baby," he slobbered drunkenly. When I heard this I tried to end the conversation. I knew he was getting serious and I also knew he could make me do it, and I was terrified of getting caught. I didn't want to kidnap a baby. Luckily he said no more on the subject. It didn't really worry me that he had suggested it—I just went along with almost everything he wanted. But I was worried about the way he would make me carry out all the crimes, then use them against me as a threat to make me keep on doing what he wanted.

We had a very volatile relationship. I allowed him to dominate me in return for his love, but I hated him touching me—yet I accepted it. That night he took out his gun and slept with it. As I lay awake I wondered if my life would ever change. I knew I had to get off the drugs but I just couldn't stop. My mind felt like it was going crazy.

John was still fairly drunk when he woke up, and he began telling me that he was planning to do something, and that he wouldn't tell me what it was until he felt like it. I made him a cup of tea and he gave me my pills. I began to panic because I knew whatever it was involved me. He kept me in suspense for three hours, until he saw how I was shaking, and then he told me that he wanted me to find another teenage girl to help me carry out thefts. He said he wanted to help me, but I knew there was more to it. I knew he would touch another girl and abuse her. I told him a boy would be better, because doing break-ins was hard. A boy would be able to handle kicking down doors easier than a girl.

"No fuckin' boys, it's a girl or nothing," he said. He was so jealous of other males coming near me—he often threatened to blow off the head of anyone who looked at me. After this I talked to a few girls I met, but none of them wanted to travel. I told John to leave it until we got to Sydney, and he agreed.

After that night on the Murrumbidgee I knew we should never park in such an isolated spot again. I was really worried that he might start one of his arguments when he was drunk and lying on a loaded gun, the way he'd slept there. He could fly off the handle in a split second—it didn't take much to upset him. I was worried that he might either shoot me or someone else. Now he decided that we should spend the rest of the trip getting as much money as we could. I knew that most of it would go down his throat. The only times John would buy me something was when I needed tampons or more Valium. I only had two pairs of jeans and my school dresses, which he made me wear all the time.

Just outside Mildura we were stopped by the police. "Can I see your licence, sir?" asked the police officer.

"What are you pulling me over for?" John asked.

"It's just a routine check—I'd like to have a look in your boot." The cop checked the car, but he can't have looked too closely, because John still had a shotgun in there. After the search was over the cop started asking John questions about me. He wanted to know who we were, where we'd come from and where we were going. He seemed satisfied with our responses, but John took this as a bad sign and decided to drive non-stop to Sydney. He gave me another twenty pills and I fell into a deep sleep.

When I woke up John told me it was one o'clock in the morning. He said we'd been driving for ten hours and were almost in Sydney. I felt really excited—finally, I thought, I would get some proper treatment. I stayed awake and looked at all the lights. We must have been near Liverpool—I remember seeing heaps of car yards. I had finally reached my destination: I felt like shouting it out to the whole world. It was a pretty big feat for me. Before I met John I had never been out of Perth. As we drove into Sydney we both smiled, even John seemed happy, and I thought it was all going to be great. But it soon proved to be the same old thing and my happiness rapidly diminished. We were out of petrol, out of money, and that meant the next step was Kings Cross.

In Dusseldorf,
Germany, I went
out collecting
Easter eggs for
my Dad — not a
bad haul, either. I
remember trying
to eat them ...
but they were
made of wood.

John and I outside our apartment in
Perth. I was feeling really angry,
because John just told me we were
leaving WA and going on the run.

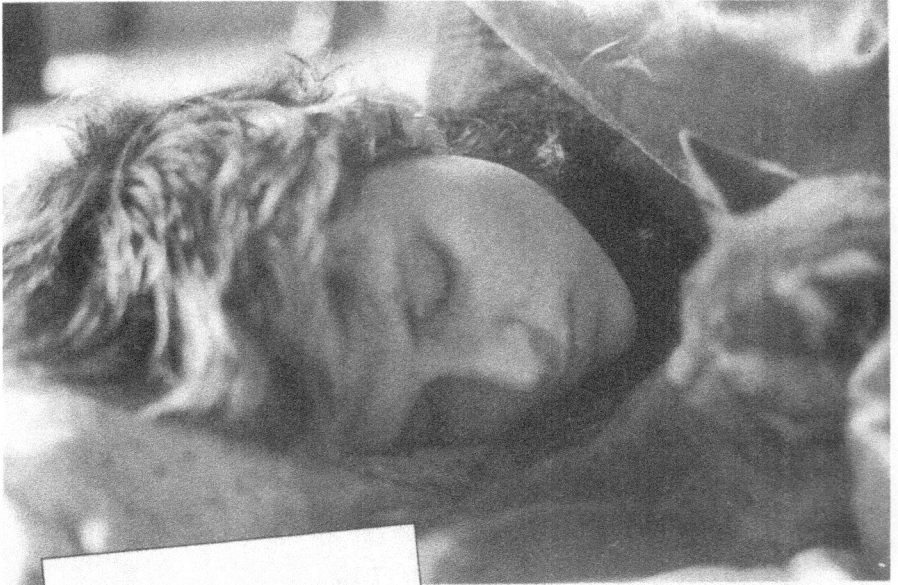

James said I looked
"angelic" in this photo ...
funny how people only
used that word to
describe me when I was
asleep. I was probably
dreaming about my new
life with James.

Modern day Robin Hoods: Tony and I outside Dee Why Social Security office. We were contemplating robbing the place ... but decided against it when we realised we'd be taking from the poor.

Playing soldiers with a friend. I used To dream aboJT escaping To faraway lands, buT in reality my life was a mess. Playing soldiers gave me self-conTrol. I did apply To join The Army, buT iT wasn't quiTe ready for me.

All These leTTers were senT
To me by Aaron, an
American soldier. I was
sixTeen and he was my
FirsT real love. I wanTed To
sTow away aboard ship To
The US, buT never quiTe
made iT.

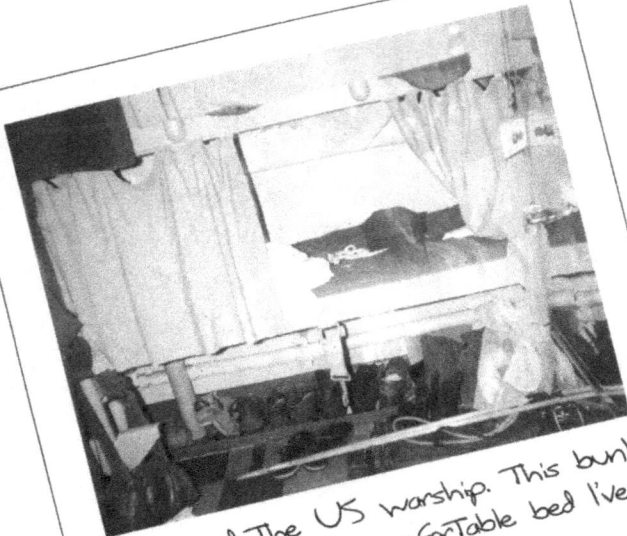

On board The US warship. This bunk was The most uncomfortable bed I've ever slept in. To all would-be stowaways: Think Twice — if The seasickness doesn't kill you, The bed will.

Minda DeTenTion CenTre, Sydney: In my room with my little rabbit "Snowball", which The staff gave me To Try To Tame me. AfTer ThaT failed, They all went out on strike.

In my convent bedroom in New Zealand I sat drinking Scotch and having a pill party ... I had just stolen a bag full of pills.

Smile for The camera &
        NoT a good Time . . .

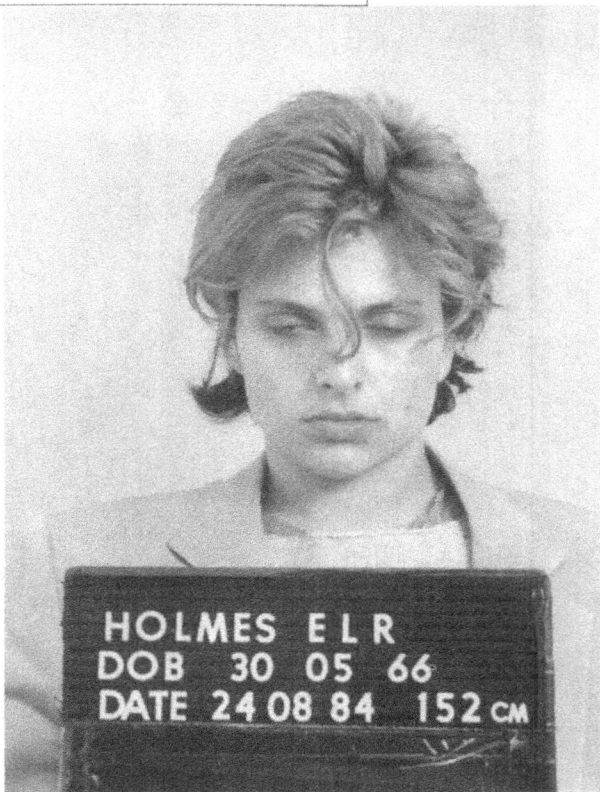

HOLMES E L R
DOB 30 05 66
DATE 24 08 84 152 CM

sydney-and brisbane

❧

1 August 1986 was a day that changed my life. As soon as we got to Kings Cross, John ordered me onto the streets to earn money. I was surrounded by girls selling their bodies. The whole place was so depressing; it had elements of sadness, poverty and death. I stood on the pavement next to a group of women who looked to be in their thirties. Some of them were barely covered, wearing only skimpy camisoles. They were trying to earn a few dollars to buy drugs and support themselves. It seemed utterly degrading.

As I stood there two burly policemen stopped beside me and asked my name. They had picked me out because I looked so young. "How old are you?" one of them asked me. I wasn't sure what to say. I was now nearly twenty, but John had always told the authorities I was sixteen. That solved many problems and gave him the control he loved. "Eighteen," I told them.

"Bullshit," said the copper.

"Er-okay, twenty," I screamed out.

"Yeah, love, and I'm Freddy Kruger—you look to me like you're sixteen at most."

"Look," I wailed. "I'm only standing here waiting for my dad." The cops didn't believe a word I said. "Look," I said, pointing, "there he is now." John waved to me and the police walked over to the car. My heart was doing a thousand beats a minute.

"Dad, Dad, they don't believe I'm eighteen!" I yelled.

The police asked John my name and my age, and he told them I was eighteen and that I was there waiting for him. The cops let me go with a warning.

"How could you fuckin' let those bastards get you!" John roared at me.

I had begun to feel sick; all the drugs in my system were knocking me about. "John, we've got nowhere to go—can I go to the Royal North Shore Hospital? Please, I really want treatment."

"What about me?" he bellowed, "you're not leaving me!"

"Well, you come too," I told him. "At least we'll have a place to sleep."

John didn't argue with this plan, he said he would tell the doctor he had heart trouble. "But it's only for one night," he yelled. "Tomorrow we're leaving!"

He drove across the Harbour Bridge, parked the car at the hospital and told me that unless we were both admitted I couldn't stay. I saw the doctor first, and told him about my panic attacks, agoraphobia and Valium addiction. He took one look at me and I was admitted. Then John was examined, and they told him could come back as an outpatient. Iheard him swearing at the doctor, demanding to be admitted.

It wasn't easy for me, Iwas so emotionally attached to John and so dependent on him, but I really wanted to get off the pills. The doctor told John I was very sick and needed treatment. My weight was borderline anorexic and I was eating pills like candy. John told me I could only stay one night; he said if I ran away or told the doctors the truth he would blow my head off. He said he was going to sleep in the car outside, and would be watching me.

I was petrified at getting off Valium and Normison. I had been taking huge amounts of them every day for a long time and my body was wrecked. I knew that in order to come off the drugs I would have to stay in hospital at least three weeks. The doctor placed me in the Cummins Unit, for psychiatric patients, and I went to bed. But I was too apprehensive to sleep and walked towards the nurses' office. I wanted to tell them about John, but my emotional attachment to him was too strong and I was afraid to let go. Instead, I walked on down to the craft room, where I was introduced to a young boy called Torry.

There was something about Torry I liked straight away. I told him why I was there, and he seemed to understand everything I said. Then I listened to his story. He was only sixteen but he had already attempted suicide. He told me he had problems at home and had slashed his wrists because he didn't know how to handle things. It felt so weird—for the first time in ages I had found someone close to my age who understood the way I felt. I showed him the scars on my arms, and even though I'd just met him, he made me promise that I wouldn't cut myself again.

We talked and talked for the rest of the day. I looked at his blue eyes and blond hair and I saw the angel in him. I felt I'd known him for years, that he was my soul-mate. Torry told me I had to get away from John, but it wasn't that simple. I knew John would be there first thing in the morning, and I was worried about him meeting Torry, because I knew he would be jealous and all hell would break loose.

The nurses in the Cummins Unit were nice. They really cared about their patients. One of the younger nurses put me to bed and gave me some Dilantin to prevent fits. I began to hang out for Valium—I knew I wasn't going to be able to handle the withdrawal.

During the night I woke shaking. I felt a huge wave of panic sweep over me, so I searched through my bag and found one sleeping pill. As I swallowed it I cried. I felt so guilty. I wanted someone to hold me and tell me I was going to be all right. I found my razor blade and began to cut my arms. The feelings inside me were so strong. Cutting my arms seemed to take that pain away, but it also added to my misery. I was a failure,

I told myself. I couldn't even kill my self properly and I was too scared to get better. My world was filled with sadness. As I lay in my hospital bed next morning, I thought about my life and wondered why I had to suffer so much. I felt anger and hate towards my mother. I kept asking myself why she never loved me or held me. I hated myself as much as I hated her. Then Torry came in, and I hid my arm. He gave me his Walkman and I played Prince's "Purple Rain" … and I knew that was where I wanted to be.

I met a few other patients, including Peter, who had shot himself in the stomach. Everyone around me was depressed, and it rubbed off on me. I talked to Torry for a while, then asked him to leave me by myself. I walked to one corner of the craft room and slashed my wrists. I knew there was no hope for me. The sight of the blood didn't bother me—as always, it felt as though my depression was flowing out with it. For some reason the song "Purple Rain" seemed like a suicide call to me. I had listened to the song over and over again and had started to believe the words.

At that moment John walked in and saw the blood. He slapped me. "What are ya doing, ya fuckin' stupid bitch! They'll keep you in here forever!" He only cared about himself. "Here, take these," he said, giving me about twenty Valium. I gobbled them down like a child eating lollies.

I introduced Torry to John, who told him to keep away from me, otherwise he'd shoot him. Torry told him he was only a friend. John knew the hospital staff were watching me closely and he decided I could stay for a short while longer, but he came back to see me every day and gave me heaps more drugs.

It took about a week for the staff to realise I was taking other medication. The nurses told me that if I continued they would stop John from coming to see me. It was so hard, I really wanted to be free, but there wasn't anyone who really cared except John. When life got tough, he was the only one there.

Then Torry was discharged, and I knew I'd go insane without his company. I would have liked to be with him, but his mother took him home to Wollongong. He told me to call him when I left hospital, but I knew John would never let me see him again.

I told John I was ready to leave the hospital—I didn't really want to, but there didn't seem much of an alternative. I asked him to pick me up next morning. After he left I swallowed every pill I had, then I walked outside. I found the railway track and decided I had to die. I felt a deep anger and so much hatred for everyone who had ever been part of my life. I put on the headphones, slashed my wrist and jumped onto the tracks. I walked towards a tunnel and lay down, listening to "Purple Rain" and praying to God to help me. Slowly I blacked out. Later I learned that a railway worker spotted me lying on the tracks and called an ambulance. I was taken back to the hospital.

I woke to find a nurse taking my blood pressure. I wanted her to hold me, I needed reassurance and love, but there was no one. I can't remember my mother ever hugging or kissing me; I had been totally starved of love throughout my entire life. I craved attention and it had reached the point where I didn't care what I did to achieve it.

"You're a very stupid girl, Roxanne," the head sister told me. "If this kind of behaviour continues you will be discharged."

"Fuck off!" I yelled. Why couldn't anyone ever understand my misery?

The psychiatrist came to see me. It was rather like talking to a brick wall. "So, how are you today, Roxanne?"

"Real good," I replied sarcastically.

"That's the shot," he said and patted me on the head. "If there is any more drug taking outside, or if you take any more Valium from your stepfather, you will be immediately discharged."

After that inspiring conversation I decided to discharge myself. It was just too hard being away from John. When he walked into the hospital right on visiting hours, I told him I was discharging myself.

"What did I say? These bastards don't know a bloody thing," he said. I felt he was right—it didn't seem as though I had accomplished much in there, or so I kept telling myself. I still had painful stitches in my arm and the doctors kept telling me I was a stupid little girl. They were right about one thing: I was a little girl, looking for love.

John decided the best thing for us was to stay in Sydney for a while. I really wanted to see Torry, but of course John wouldn't let me. So we hung out in a motel in Chatswood for a few days. We were down to our last few dollars, and the motel wanted their money. Finally the manager said if we didn't pay up we'd have to leave. I called Torry and asked him if he could lend me some money. He agreed, so John decided we could now drive to Wollongong. We found Torry's place, and John told me to go in—but he said that if I tried any funny business he would blow the door down. Torry invited me in and I begged him to come with me.

"Roxanne, I'll only come if you get rid of John," he said. "Torry, he's got a gun. And—I need him. Just come, please," I begged.

At that moment John appeared. "Come on, Roxanne, we've got to leave," he said.

"John, Torry's coming with us." John looked at me like he was going to explode. I told Torry I needed to talk to John alone, and we walked outside. "Look, I really think Torry will be able to help us," I told him. "He's better than me at breaking into places, he'll protect us from the cops."

John finally agreed, but he warned me that there would be no funny business between me and Torry, otherwise Torry would get hurt. Torry said goodbye to his parents and we all headed off. Once on the road, John warned Torry: "If ya fuckin' get caught by the cops, keep ya trap shut." He told him that the coppers would play games to get a conviction at all costs and that he should say fuck all.

I didn't know where we were heading, until John suggested we should take a look at sunny Queensland. I knew it wasn't going to be any holiday—more like another week of breaking into houses and shops. Torry tried his best not to upset John. We rarely talked when John was in one of his moods, and most of the trip was quiet and boring.

I was depressed and needed food. John kept giving us both pills which bombed us out.

By the time we arrived in Brisbane our car looked like it had been through a mud slide. It was less than fifteen minutes before the cops pulled us over. I was in no mood to be asked a thousand and one questions. John went through all the questions and answers and the cop said we weren't allowed to drive the car because it had defects.

I'd had it. For some reason I just can't explain I told the cop to fuck off.

"Who do you fuckin' think you're swearing at!" the cop shouted at me.

"You, pig-face!" I blurted out. Then I stuck my finger up at him, and we were all under arrest.

Because John had outstanding warrants in Sydney he was taken to the watch-house, and we went with him. I knew I was in deep shit, and that it was all my own fault.

"God, Torry, what have I done?" Most of the time I was so drugged that I didn't understand my own behaviour. All I kept thinking now was I wanted John back so we could go home... wherever that was.

At the Brisbane watch-house John performed his well practised fake heart-attack, and was rushed to one of the city hospitals. Torry was released into a hostel, and I remained in the watch-house. I still had a spare bottle of pills on me and I knew I would have to swallow them to be free. Funnily enough, I never thought about dying, only about being with John again.

Torry, meanwhile, had decided to tell the police all about John and the criminal things he made me do. They immediately called a woman from the Department of Community Services. At last the authorities began to understand what was really going on. By this time I had swallowed all the pills and cut my wrists again, and I was rushed to the same hospital as John.

"Wake up, sweetheart." Was I in heaven? Then the nurse demanded a urine sample and the walls came tumbling down. I knew I wasn't going to die, I'd only taken about twenty sleeping pills, but I still felt pretty sick. I thought back to the time when I was fourteen and had managed to meet Michael Jackson, my idol, when he visited Perth. Michael had had a traumatic past. Now I told myself that he'd been able to pull through it all, and so could I. Thinking about him gave me some hope.

The nurses and doctors around me didn't know anything about me, we were like ships that pass in the night. Once again I felt that John was my rock. "Where's my dad!" I screamed at the nurse, who told me he was very sick. I knew he wasn't, but I didn't want to spoil his plan. I had to get dressed and find him. I managed to get into my clothes and took off along the corridor, feeling extremely groggy.

John was in a single room, so I knew he would find it easy to escape. "What are we going to do?" I asked him.

"Don't worry, I'm getting out. I want you to leave now and I'll meet you outside in half an hour."

"Roxanne, where have you been? Get back into bed." The nurse had found me wandering along the corridor and now she guided me back to the ward. A social worker was on her way to see me. As I lay in bed I tried to think of ways to escape and for John, Torry and me to be together again.

"Hello, Roxanne, I'm the social worker. I've been speaking to Torry and he has told me about your life with John. He also told me that John tried to molest him in various ways. We want to help you both."

"He's lying," I said. "Anyway, I don't want to talk to you." I tried to get rid of her so that I could get out, but she wouldn't leave.

"Look, Roxanne, we know John has been molesting you and we know it's not your fault. If we're to charge him you've got to make a statement." She tried to convince me to have John charged, but I didn't want to. I hated dealing with tough issues, I had never been good at facing reality. It was so much easier to run away from myself and the world.

"Torry has decided to make a statement, and we'd like you to help us," she went on. "How would you feel if John went out there and molested another child, much younger?" And she reached out and put her arm around me.

"Get away from me!" I yelled. I distrusted any show of affection because I wasn't used to it. "Fuck off!" I screamed as I pushed her away. "Get out of here, I don't want to listen to you."

"Roxanne, I'm going to pick you up in an hour, and Torry's coming too."

"Where are we going?"

"Well, I'd like you to speak to another doctor at a different hospital, who deals with issues like this."

"ISSUES!" I yelled. ""m not coming!"

At this point she walked out of the room. I had tried to be as horrible to her as I could. I liked people hating me, it was my defence against them. If they didn't like me then they wouldn't try to get too close to me. A young nurse came in and tried to convince me I should go. I couldn't escape because they were all watching me too closely.

Sure enough, Sue, the social worker, returned exactly one hour later. All I could think about was John, and trying to find him. Sue picked up Torry along the way and drove us a short distance to the other hospital. It was a children's hospital, so I knew it wouldn't be too long before the Welfare tried to take me away. The doctor there seemed nice but I told Torry not to say anything, otherwise we'd both end up in a locked home.

"Rox, I really love you," he told me. "We don't need John, we'll be okay."

"I hate you, Torry, how could you do this? I know what John did, but he didn't mean it. He really likes you—come on, I don't want to be around the stupid Welfare, let's find John." Torry realised I wouldn't leave John, so he finally agreed not to have him charged, and we were driven back to the first hospital. Before Sue dropped Torry off I asked him where he was staying.

"It's a psych hospital," he told me. "I tried to cut my wrists because of what John did." He gave me the number to get in touch with him.

All the way back Sue kept trying to persuade me to make a statement, but I wouldn't.

I knew I had to find John. I wanted outta the hospital. At last I managed to get away and found John in the carpark, where he had been faithfully waiting for me. He asked me what I'd said to the social worker.

"I never dobbed you in, it was bloody Torry, he's told them what you did."

"And what was that?" he shouted.

"Look," I howled, they took us to this hospital and asked us about you but I didn't say anything. God, John, can I please have something to calm my nerves?"

He gave me three pills and I finally relaxed.

"Look, Rox," he said, "where is Torry? We've got to find him and get out of this fucking state."

I told him where Torry was and we drove to the hospital. It's funny, you can always spot a psychiatric hospital, they're always as old as the convicts. It wasn't difficult for Torry to walk out and join us.

"You'll be fuckin' sorry if you said anything!" John bellowed at him. "I'll fuckin' blow ya brains out if I go down on this one."

Reduced to tears, Torry told him the cops had wanted to know every detail, and he'd only talked because he was scared. I could tell that Torry was scared stiff of John.

It was time to leave Brisbane. I knew that John was raging inside. We drove for some twenty kilometres, then he pulled over onto a dirt track and ordered Torry and me out of the car.

"Roxanne, get your fucking face here now!" he shouted. I jumped out and he handed me the gun. "Now shoot Torry, you bitch. No one ever double-crosses me."

I was horrified. "I can't," I cried, "please don't make me." "Give me the goddam gun." He grabbed it from me and slapped me across the face.

Torry was nearly shitting himself. "Get yer fuckin' gear off, fuckface," John told him.

Torry quickly took off all his clothes. I knew John could be crazy, but there was no way I was going to sit back and let Torry die. "Throw ya fuckin' gear into the car!" he shouted, then he ordered Torry to walk back to Sydney and yelled at me to get in the car. He got in himself and started the engine. It was like living with a psychopath; you never knew what mood John would be in next. Then something snapped and he reversed his decision. He threw Torry's clothes at him and ordered him back into the car.

"Okay, you two, enough of the piss-farting around, the money situation is fuckin' low, ya gunna hit at the next spot. So get ya shit together—and remember, the next one who fucks up will taste a bullet up their arse."

After about quarter of an hour's drive John pulled up

outside a small country town, parking in a spot where none of the shopkeepers could see us. He ordered Torry out of the car and shoved a few pills into my mouth. "Roxanne," he whispered, "you know I do love you and no bastard will ever take you away from me. That's why I gotta do this." He went to the car boot, took out some rope, then seized me and tied my hands together. It hurt like hell. After this he told Torry he was to rob a store he had picked out, taking the rifle with him. He pulled Torry closer and said that if he fucked this job up he, John, would kill me.

I could see Torry was really scared. He thought the only way to keep me alive was to go along with it. John wrote out a demand note and handed the sawn-off shotgun to Torry. "You've got two minutes, or else you'll never see your mate again," John told him. Torry ran off to the store, the gun concealed under his shirt.

"Please, John, don't make him do it, we'll get caught, don't make him!" I howled.

I tried to run from the car but John had tied my hands too tightly. He slapped me across the face again. I know now how badly he treated me, but back then I truly thought he loved me. All my life I had been abused; to me this was normal behaviour.

The next two minutes seemed to last forever. My heart pounded and I sweated profusely—not for myself but for Torry. I knew that if he didn't succeed he was finished. At last he came bolting back towards us.

"RIGHT" John bellowed. He revved the motor and we took off at high speed.

"So what did we get?" he yelled.

Torry opened the bag. There was at least $300. We knew we had to get out of this place fast, otherwise we'd be done for. John's motto was to live the life of a "free spirit." He knew the cops would be lying in wait for us at the next town. He looked at the map and saw a small township about eighty kilometres down the track. When we reached it he made a detour into the bush. "Right, off with the ropes," he told me, and untied my hands with a knife. "Now, off with your clothes." I stripped and he ordered me to put on my old school uniform. Then he lit a campfire and burnt my clothes and Torry's.

We camped there overnight. John let me sleep while he and Torry spray-painted the car. John always kept cans of spray paint when we travelled. Next morning I woke to find our cream-coloured car was now bright blue. John and Torry were still fast asleep. I was hungry, and decided to take a look in the boot, but there was nothing to eat—just spare clothes, camping equipment and enough ammunition for a federal assault.

I wasn't feeling well. When John woke I asked him if we could get some food. I remarked that Torry had done well, and for the first time in weeks he agreed with me, and said we could feed at the next shop we came to. As we drove off I felt nervous. I always had this nagging feeling that John would be taken away and I'd be left alone. I was very much a child trapped in a nineteen-year-old body.

return to sydney

❦

We never did get caught for that robbery. We drove straight down the east coast of Australia in twelve hours—not a bad record. Once we hit the New South Wales border we all breathed sighs of relief. Each state border we passed seemed like a celebration for John. He would get totally pissed—and that worried me.

In Sydney, John suggested we make for Kings Cross. I knew he wanted me to work chatting up guys and conning them. I hated the way he would send me onto the street. I truly loathed it from the depths of my soul, it went against all my dreams of someday being part of a family. We soon found our way to the Cross, with those bright lights, that huge Coke sign and all the young girls selling their bodies to desperate middle-aged men who wanted to use and abuse them. The sadness of the scene reflected the way I felt.

We checked into a hotel in the heart of the Cross. "Right, Rox, you've got two seconds to make your face up, get dressed and onto the street," John told me.

I didn't have many clothes, so I wore my old school uniform, a blue skirt and white shirt. Standing on the street reminded me of Hindley Street in Adelaide, and I began to question myself. Why was I standing there—was I incapable of any rational thought? I recalled one time back in England when I was about five. I'd almost fallen from a great height in a derelict building, and I remembered how my mother grab bed my hand as I slipped. I suppose I was always looking for another hand to save me, but I never seemed to find one.

Suddenly I felt a touch on my shoulder. I heard the sound of a police radio and the reality of a cold night in Kings Cross hit me.

"What's your name? How old are you?" asked the police officer.

"Twenty-one," I told him.

"Don't spin me that crap, you're not a day over fifteen. What are you doing?"

"I'm just waiting for my dad." John was parked across the road, as usual—he always kept me in sight. "Look, there he is." I pointed towards the car.

"Okay," said the cop. "But move on now. If I catch you here again I'm locking you up."

I ran over to the car, and John said it was too dangerous for me to work here. Instead, he sent Torry onto the street to solicit guys.

I spent the night sitting in the car as John went on drinking. We sat and waited for hours. I was really tired. I asked if I could go to sleep, but John told me it was my job to watch Torry. Torry wasn't any better at picking up than I was. Finally I told John it was a waste of time and he agreed. He ordered me to go over and tell Torry to get his act together, otherwise he would take off to Perth with me, leaving him right there.

I walked back to the street, and as I joined Torry I saw the same two police ofticers coming back. I gripped Torry's hand and the police thought I was picking him up. They told me they wanted to see some ID, otherwise I would be locked up. They also grabbed Torry, and he blurted out that John had been abusing him and me for ages, and had threatened to kill us if we told anyone. All this time I knew John would be getting really angry, seeing what was going on. I knew that if Torry said any more we were both gone. I ran over to the car and told John that the police were questioning Torry.

After taking our details from Torry, finally the cops said we were free to go, but if they saw us again we would be sent to a juvenile detention centre, and that we wouldn't be able to handle that. I felt like telling them that I'd spent almost all my childhood in the fucking places, but I had the sense to realise that they would then know I'd been in trouble.

John knew we couldn't hang around any longer, so he took us back to the hotel. I was exhausted. John wouldn't allow me to share Torry's bed, so I ended up sleeping with him. I fell asleep pretty quickly, thanks to all the pills he'd given me.

Torry had given the police the name of our hotel, and around midnight I woke to a huge noise as police, Welfare workers and detectives stormed into our room. They dragged John out of bed and led him away for questioning. Then they asked me whether he had been molesting me. I denied everything. John and I had a code of silence and he had told me exactly what I should say if this situation ever arose:

"My full name is Roxanne Darton."

"Your age?"

"Sixteen. Where have you taken my dad? I'm not telling you anything—fuck off."

I hated the Welfare, they had always condemned me, never helped me. I blamed them for everything.

Torry and I were then bundled into a car and taken to an office somewhere in the city. The police had taken John into custody after questioning him.

"We believe your dad has been having an incestuous relationship with you," one of the Welfare officers told me. "We know he hurts you and we want you to tell us about it so that we can help you."

I never wanted to be separated from John, I refused to believe that what he was doing was wrong. I didn't tell them anything, and finally they took Torry and me back to the hotel, saying they would come back to collect us in the morning and take us somewhere else. The Kings Cross police escorted us back to the hotel.

As soon as we were alone, I told Torry I was going out to find John.

"But Roxanne, he hurts you, he's dangerous," Torry protested.

I needed Valium to drown out his words. The ten pills I took didn't seem to do me any good. We were running out of money again and there was no way I was going anywhere with those Welfare workers. I told Torry I was going to sleep in the car, and we both ended up doing that.

I woke up very early. After the huge surge of adrenalin it had received, my rigid body felt like it was ready to do battle. I told Torry I would go and carry out a robbery. After all, my greatest heroes were Ben Hall and Ned Kelly, so why shouldn't I follow their example? Torry protested, but I said I wanted to do the job because I couldn't stand the thought of him getting caught and taken away from me. He was my only friend now. In the end we decided to do it together.

That evening Torry drove the car to St Leonards, which was bustling with traffic and brightly lit. We parked the car in the train station carpark, and I found the gun and a cloth bag for the loot. Torry pulled on a balaclava. His wrists were still bandaged from the time he had tried to commit suicide in Adelaide. (Later, the police were to call us "The Bandage Men".) He kissed me on the cheek and we ran into a chemist's shop we had marked out.

"This is a fucking stick-up, hit the fuckin' floor!" I shouted.

Torry held the gun, half-concealed, and I threw the bag at the petrified woman behind the counter. Torry told me to go and start the car—it was all over in a few minutes. I revved up the car, he jumped in and we took off towards Artarmon. As we drove further along eight police cars came screaming along the

Pacific Highway...in pursuit of armed robbers. We laughed, not at what we had done, just the way it had take the police ten minutes to respond. The job had netted only $200 and we knew we had to get more. For one thing, the car needed fixing and that would cost a lot.

We drove around Artarmon. The only shops now open were all-night chemists, and we thought it might be better not to hit another of those. But then Torry yelled out: "That's it, Roxy!" He'd spotted a perfectly situated all-night chemist's shop. As we pulled in we saw there was a young girl at the counter. We jumped out to survey the shop properly and I gave Torry the go-ahead. He jumped the counter and pointed the gun straight at the girl.

"Don't shoot me!" she cried.

"Just fill the fucking bag—I want the lot, don't fuck with the silver, just the notes." I didn't even consider the girl's feelings—I only knew I too was the victim of a cruel world. Torry grabbed the loot and we took off at high speed.

We decided to change our clothes and pulled off the highway into a street about a kilometre from the shop. I put on my school dress and Torry pulled on a pair of jeans. We looked sweet and innocent. Torry moved across to kiss me, and at that moment a car stopped beside us.

"Fuck, Torry, cops!" I hissed.

Two uniformed policemen approached our car. What else could we do...I grabbed Torry and we kissed.

"That will be enough of that," said the cop.

"But officer," I protested, "we're not doing anything wrong. We're out on our first date together."

"Where have you been?" the cop demanded.

"Robbing banks, what do you think!" I told him. 'Just leave us alone."

All the while I had over $1000 sitting there between my legs.

"What's going on?" Torry asked in a concerned voice. "There's so many police cars about—has someone been murdered?"

The copper shook his head. "Some asshole has just robbed a store up the road. He was dressed in black, a real heavy type."

As he said that a message came over the radio: *All cars be on the lookout for a male aged about twenty, dubbed "Bandage Man," has bandages on both arms.*

"Okay, kids, you'd better be on your way," the cop told us. "There's a maniac running around here with a loaded gun."

The next three days were fantastic. We decided to stay at the Sydney Hilton. We had a warm bed and hot showers, and ate food I'd never tasted before. Torry and I decided that having a good time was more important than keeping our money, so we hired a chauffeured limousine, went to the Cross and picked up five stray winos. Then we told the driver to return to the Hilton and took our guests into the restaurant there. All through dinner they burped, farted, dribbled, slobbered their food and had the waiters running right, left and centre…It was the best night and we all got something out of it. Afterwards, our five winos followed us up to our room and decided to raid the bar fridge of its entire contents. We were all pretty drunk, and I was also taking pills.

Around two o'clock in the morning there was a lot of noise in the corridor and the management stormed the place. Apparently some posh bitch next door had complained about us. We were all ordered to leave the premises.

Once again Torry and I were out on the streets and didn't know what to do. We considered admitting ourselves into the Royal North Shore Hospital, but I knew I would be questioned about all the slashes on my arms. Having a psychiatric history is no laughing matter.

Torry and I really did love each other. He was the strong

side of me. Maybe we were a sort of extension of each other. I knew that I didn't really want to be locked up again, but where could we go?

"Maybe we should to to Mum's place in Wollongong," Terry said at last.

I thought that wasn't such a bad idea. I had met his mother once before and she'd seemed quite nice. I took the guns and some ammunition from the car and we parked in a motel carpark at Artarmon. Then Torry and I caught the train to Wollongong and his mum picked us up. Her house was right behind the station. She insisted on calling me "darling" and referred to me as her "daughter". I disliked that. I guess I had become so used to being abused that I only felt comfortable when it was going on. We arrived late at night. I swallowed the last of my Valium and tried to get to sleep. But somehow I didn't feel safe in that house; I was haunted by the thought that no one would ever really love me.

I couldn't relax. I got up and asked Torry if he wanted to come and shoot some bullets onto the railway tracks— it would be a way for me to release my stress. I picked up John's .22 rifle and took heaps of ammunition. Then Torry and I went outside…and I headed into trouble. We found a nice quiet spot at the back of the house and I began to fire the gun into the air. With each shot my anger and hatred of all the people who had wrecked my life came pouring out. The fourteen or so Valium pills I'd taken were making me feel thoroughly disillusioned.

"Come on, Rox, we'd better go," Torry said. "We'll wake Mum—if we haven't done that already."

As Torry went off I decided to stay. I felt I needed to be alone. This was Torry's family, not mine. I knew that if I started to care deeply about someone I would only get hurt again. I wanted to build a bigger, stronger wall around myself.

I found an old railway worker's shed and sat down. My head was spinning. I began to cry—I wanted to escape from my pain. Was I really so bad? I needed someone to put their arms around me and tell me everything was going to be okay.

I felt like I was nothing. Sitting there in the shed made reality hit home.

A voice broke the silence. "Come on, love, give me the gun."

A man was standing in the doorway. *Fuck*, I thought, *there's no way I'm going to be locked up, I'd rather be dead.* "Come and shoot me!" I screamed, "I don't care!"

I picked up the gun and fired a shot that went right between my toes. Why I didn't blast my foot to smithereens I'll never know.

"Listen, love, I've got a magnum and I'll shoot if you don't give me that gun." The guy was a railway worker.

I picked up the gun, reloaded, and said: "I'm not coming out. If you want me you'll have to shoot me!"

The next thing the place was swarming with cops. Someone had heard the shots and called the police. "Come out, kid, or we'll have to force you out!" I knew they were serious, and when I stuck my head out there was the SWOS team—the Special Weapons and Operations Squad. "Come on, sweetheart, no one's going to hurt you. Just come out and we'll take care of your problems."

How could they possibly sort out my life? It was a mess. I'd been slashing my wrists since I was thirteen. My problems were so complex that even the world's most brilliant psychiatrist would be at a loss.

"Listen, sweetie," said the SWOS officer, "what do you want?"

I couldn't believe they were asking this. What did they expect me to answer—a mum and dad, a million bucks, dial-a-pizza? In answer I told them to fuck off. "None of you can help me! If I come out you'll shoot me." I was pretty drugged, but I knew I had to get out of this alive. There had always been a faint religious ember burning inside me, and now I prayed.

"Please, God, don't let anyone hurt me. I'm going out, but please don't let them hurt me."

The SWOS officer told me to drop the gun and two policemen helped me from the hut. One of them, who would have been about my dad's age, put his arm around me and told me everything would be okay and at that moment I believed him.

In fact the Wollongong police were really nice to me after all I'd put them through. They told me I was just a sick girl and that they'd take me to hospital. As the ambulance drove to Wollongong Hospital it seemed that nothing had changed. I was a lost child craving love, but the only attention I ever got was from the police, the medicos and the courts.

I was placed in the psychiatric ward and held down by three nurses who gave me a huge shot of Largactil and Serenace, powerful anti-psychotic and sedative drugs. I hated being forced to have these drugs. I realised my behaviour wasn't normal, but then my whole life had been abnormal.

After three days of medical abuse I escaped from the hospital and went back to Torry's place. There was no one at home: afterwards I learned that he had tried to commit suicide again because he thought he couldn't live without me. His folks had taken him to Sydney to be admitted to the Royal North Shore Hospital. I climbed through a window, got my clothes and some more ammunition. Just as I was about to leave I heard a police car and an ambulance draw up outside, and a cop knocking on the door. When no one answered they left, and a little while afterwards so did I.

I caught the first available train to Sydney and went straight to the Royal North Shore Hospital. In the psychiatric ward they told me that Torry wasn't allowed visitors. I felt then that I really need John, and I called his friend Jill. She told me he was still in custody and applying for bail. I knew I couldn't help him—I would have had to hold up a bank to get his bail money. Besides, I was now beginning to get massive withdrawal symptoms. With my last twenty dollars I walked into the North Sydney Cellars and bought a bottle of bourbon. I had a plan, and this time I was determined to stick to it.

Quickly I drank almost the whole bottle of bourbon, then wrote a suicide note, telling my mum how much I loved her. I wrote that I had forgiven my parents, so that they would not feel too guilty about me. Finally I walked onto the North Sydney railway line, put on my headphones and waited to die. I kept singing Prince's "Purple Rain" and then lay down and passed out for what seemed hours, but was really only a few moments.

As I heard later, a railway employee was informed that a female had been seen walking on the tracks, and they stopped all the trains. I was eventually found, unconscious. I recall waking and seeing police all around me. One thing was sure: they weren't angels, so I knew I hadn't died and gone to heaven...maybe I was in hell!

Two cops and a doctor lifted me off the tracks and put me in an ambulance. I was taken to the Royal North Shore Hospital where I had tubes shoved down my throat and a drip put in my arm, after which I was admitted to a ward for observation. I heard one of the nurses remark that maybe I should have taken a real overdose and done a proper job. I understood her frustration but I don't think she understood mine.

Most girls of my age were worrying about how they would make up some tiff they'd had with their boyfriend; my life lurched from crisis to crisis with never-ending pain. There seemed no way out. I was glad that at least I would have the chance of seeing Torry again. I knew I could not survive alone.

"Roxanne," the nurse told me, "we are going to transfer you to Cummins Unit. We are aware of your friendship with Torry, but you are not allowed to talk to him, otherwise you will be separated from each other."

The Cummins Unit was boring with a capital B. I hated group therapy, I disliked the nurses, I loathed the way everyone was labelled. Each patient was put into a colour scheme to denote how messed up they were. For example, a red dot meant red alert. In this case you weren't allowed to wear ordinary clothes and you were considered a suicide risk. And that meant you could not go outside the unit. I had been in the Cummins Unit before, and I hated being forced into a routine. I had never adapted well to people other than John telling me what to do.

One morning I decided to try a spot of painting in the quiet room. I enjoyed painting, it released some of my stress. As I sat there I heard someone come into the room and looked around. "Torry, my God, it's really you!" I shouted.

He threw his arms around me. "Roxie, we have to get out of here. I've heard that the nurses and doctors think you are too suicidal and they're planning to send you away to a locked hospital. I think the railway overdose really did it."

"Oh Torry, what are we going to do?" I asked. "Please don't leave me."

"I'll never do that," Torry told me. "Get your stuff, we're leaving now."

We walked out of the hospital but had no idea where to go. I called the police to see if they could tell me where John was. They told me he was in custody at Long Bay Gaol, in the hospital wing. Torry and I headed back to Artarmon, to where we'd left the car, but there was no sign of it. I felt scared about leaving the vicinity of the hospital, so we slept in the hospital grounds that night, and next morning we took a bus to Chatswood.

"We either stay on the run from the cops or we give ourselves up," I told Torry. I knew that all he .wanted was my love, and all I had ever wanted was security and a family to love me, but I was aware that I had become institutionalised and couldn't cope with too much of the outside world. It scared me.

As we walked through Chatswood that evening I saw a wonderful sight—a Westpac Bank. I told Torry to wait on the footpath while I went into an alleyway. I found a brick and hurled it through one of the bank's plate-glass windows. The double security doors flew open and we walked inside.

"Wow, Torry, the bank's all ours! Stick 'em up!" I said. We waited for the alarms to start screaming but nothing happened, so we walked out again and flagged down a passing police car.

"Officer, I've just broken into the bank—arrest me!" I demanded.

"You're joking," one of the cops said, "okay, I'm arresting you!" And they drove off laughing. I tried chasing them—I couldn't believe it. The day I scream to be arrested the cops just drive away!

Torry and I stood there dazed. "Let's try to find the car, get John's gun out of the boot and hold up a bank properly," I suggested.

"Maybe we should go for a service station—banks are too risky," Torry replied.

Then I said: "Maybe we should call the cops." So we found a phone box and dialled the Chatswood police. "Look, copper, don't give me any crap," I said. "We've just broken into the Westpac bank and we want to be arrested. Hurry up, we're waiting!" The cop sounded mystified and sent a car round to investigate. I'm sure they expected to find it had been a hoax call, and were astounded to see us both waiting outside the bank with our overnight bags.

"Okay, you two little smartarses," the cops said as they flung us into the police car. We were driven to Chatswood police station, given a set of handcuffs each and a few slaps across the face, and they threw in a free interrogation as well. Torry and I were separated and placed in different interview rooms. A large detective came to see me.

"Right, full name and address?" he asked.

"Roxanne Lee Darton," I answered.

"Date of birth?" "30 August 1970."

"And where are your parents?"

I told him my father was John Darton and that he was in Long Bay prison. The detective left the room and I waited for him to return. I must admit that I was very scared. I had been bashed by the cops before and the fear of it happening again filled my mind.

"Okay, Roxanne, we know about your stepfather and Torry has told us about the robberies you both committed. Now it's your turn to cooperate with us. We're not listening to any crap. Got it?"

I sat in front of the detective with wild thoughts running through my head. Should I confess, should I lie? Maybe I should hang myself? Suddenly I realised I could be let out on bail, and then maybe I could help John. But where would the bail money come from? I knew Torry would be okay because his mother loved him and would always provide bail or surety for him.

The detective informed me that Torry had confessed and that a woman was willing to identify us both as the armed robbers. So it seemed there was no point in lying. They had enough evidence against us. The detective then asked me where the weapon was. At this point I asked whether I could visit the toilet. I had a secret stash of pills down my jeans and I wanted to take them all. A nice policewoman called Anne escorted me to the toilets—as I went inside she stood watching me, but I managed to swallow about five Valium tablets without her noticing. I asked her what was going to happen to me, but she didn't reply. I also asked the police to give me bail, but they took no notice.

Back in the interview room, I sat at a desk surrounded by five male detectives and Anne, the female constable. I opened one of the desk drawers: there, right before my eyes, was a hand-gun, a .38 Smith & Wesson. *My God*, I thought. Fearfully I grabbed the gun and looked at Anne. Before she had a chance to move, the gun was at her head. "I'm going to blow her away!"

I screamed at the five detectives. I was clearly out of control: I think the drugs in my system added to the anger inside me.

"Please don't hurt me," Anne pleaded. "I've been kind to you. Please don't hurt me!"

I looked at her. She was right. In spite of all my pain and trauma, shooting her made no sense. I hated violence. I didn't want to hurt her.

As I went on holding the gun to Anne's head, the detectives began shouting at me. "Put the gun down, Roxanne"—"Come on, be a good girl!"—"Come on, Roxanne, put it down!" Their voices rose above my own thoughts and reality hit me once again. There was no chance of escape for me. I relinquished the gun, telling the cops I wouldn't shoot Anne because she had been good to me. Anne then burst into tears and quickly left the room.

Sitting in the police station seemed an all too familiar scenario. When would things ever change? At that stage I don't think I really believed I possessed the power to change… it was all embedded too deep inside me. The police charged Torry and me with two counts of armed robbery. We were fingerprinted, photographed and questioned again. Then the Chatswood police called Torry's mother, who agreed to bail him out. She offered to bail me as well, but the police said that since she was not my next of kin, it was up to a magistrate to decide that. After this the police asked me about my relationship with John. They said they had received two notices that I was a child at risk, and they were sending me to an institution called Yasmar, so that I could be further interviewed by child protection officers.

I believe they wanted to detain me in order to find out more about John's criminal activities. Finally I was told it was time to go, and I was led, handcuffed, into a police van together with Torry. A police constable and Anne, the policewoman, were our escorts. As we drove through Sydney I knew it would be a long time before I saw the outside world again. I felt relieved to be with Torry—he had told his mum that he didn't want her to bail him out until after I appeared in court, so that we could be bailed together.

When we got out of the van at Yasmar, Torry told me he loved me and never wanted to be apart from me. We were led into a dimly lit hallway, with Anne holding onto me by the waistband of my pants. Suddenly, as she pulled at me, I turned around, grabbed the gun out of her holster and told her to freeze, threatening to shoot either myself or her. The male police officer who'd come with us was a little way ahead. He swung round as soon as he heard the female cop yell out: "Drop the gun, Roxanne!"

"I can't!" I shouted. "You're going to take Torry away from me!"

Anne must have been every bit as scared as I was myself. I don't know what possessed me to do it. I really think the Valium was probably responsible. It certainly dulled my senses.

Feeling confused, I held onto the gun for about five minutes. Why was I doing it?

"Come on, Roxanne, we're not going to hurt you. Just put down the gun, throw it along the floor over here, you won't get into any trouble," the policeman said.

"Okay, I'll put it down, but please don't hurt me," I said. Slowly I put the gun on the floor and fell to my knees. I expected to be kicked and dragged into a cell; instead I was given a sedative and put to bed.

Next morning the Yasmar staff woke me and gave me breakfast. They asked a lot of questions about my family and where I was from. They asked about John, and where my mother was. I found it difficult to keep on lying, but John had started the ball rolling when he'd first lied to the police on the Nullarbor Plain. Later in the morning I was told to get ready to be taken to Bidura Children's Court, at Glebe. I asked where Torry was and was told he would appear in court, and that I wasn't allowed to talk to him before the hearing because he was an accomplice.

At Bidura Court I was put into a caged area surrounded by police, youth workers and other kids. I knew that without John or Torry there was no way out for me. I asked a youth worker for a glass of water, then smashed the glass and slashed my wrist. "Oh God!" screamed the youth worker. "Call the doctor." Two other youth workers were trying to restrain me. My reactions to stressful situations were often totally irrational. When the doctor came I was given an injection to calm me. In reality it blotted out my emotional pain and lessened the stress of the youth workers.

The magistrate on duty was Rod Blackmore, a wonderful human being who genuinely tried to help those who came before him. It was rare to find any magistrate who put so much personal time and energy into helping so many fallen angels.

As I stood before the bench while the charges against me were read out, I heard someone mention a Care and Protection Order and I realised that the police were applying to have me admitted to Yasmar as a child at risk. I jumped up and yelled: "Get my dad! I'm not a child at risk. I hate you all—so-called Welfare has screwed up my life!" Mr Blackmore told me to calm down and the case was adjourned for two weeks so that the department could try to locate my supposed mother.

I was taken back to Yasmar and placed in a locked room. I hated being alienated—I felt the same rejection my parents had cast upon me as a child. Then two youth workers took me to the upper level of the building so see the nurse and I tried to jump off an open balcony, but the staff grabbed me and took me off to a Time-out room. Once again, being locked in a room with nothing to do was their idea of helping me. I really wanted John. I prayed that he would find me so that we could go back on the road one day. Then I decided to pay back the staff. Within minutes I had ripped out the stitches in my arm and they all came running.

The Yasmar doctor, Leanne Burton, decided that maybe Yasmar wasn't the right place for a girl like me. She told me that unless something was done about me the staff had threatened to go out on strike. Their threats didn't worry me. I was determined to make their lives as miserable as mine had been. Sometimes I wondered—if I'd had parents who loved and wanted me, would I have been different? I knew the answer was yes.

The staff at Yasmar hadn't ever had to deal with someone like me. I hurt myself at every opportunity. I refused to shower. I pulled out my stitches and banged my head against the walls. I hated myself. No one wanted to be on the shift when I attempted suicide. I wasn't allowed to talk to the other kids at Yasmar. The staff decided I needed a nurse with me twenty-four hours of the day to protect me from myself. My first guard was Melanie. I hated her with a passion. She was so smart, and so matronly. I told her to get a life. She made it quite clear that she disliked me intensely. I remember asking her whether I could go to the toilet without her watching. I hated this—it reminded me of the way John used to watch me. She told me it was her job and that she did not enjoy doing it. I grabbed her hair in frustration.

No one ever came to me and asked if I wanted to talk. No one showed me any affection. I just felt punished, dependent still on John, and I was filled with extreme fear and hate most of the time. Elizabeth Davies, the head of the Young Offenders Support Service, came to see me. She asked me where my mother was, and I told her I was from Tasmania and that John was my only living relative. She said she was going to try to find my mother and would visit me again. I thought she was okay. She brought me some new clothes. After she left I thought that maybe things weren't too bad after all.

Melanie didn't last long. Yasmar decided that another nurse would be more appropriate. What I wanted more than anything was to be allowed to talk to the other kids, to be treated normally. But then the staff decided I was to be locked in a cell until my court case came up. They put me in a room with no clothes—I wore a nightie they provided. I was strip-searched and left with just an iron-frame bed and a basin. They had taken all my jewellery in case I used it to hurt myself. Then I had an idea: perhaps I could drown myself. I stuffed the plug-hole of the basin with toilet paper and turned on the taps. Soon water ran across the floor and leaked under the door into the passage way. The staff came in and dived on top of me, pulling my hair to restrain me. Then they gave me another injection.

Next morning the staff decided I should be transferred to a psychiatric hospital. I was driven to a doctor's surgery, then taken to Rozelle Psychiatric Hospital. It was a dreadful place— to me the staff seemed madder than the patients. The doctors at Rozelle decided I was suicidal and should be placed in a locked ward. I was stripped, given pyjamas to wear, and made to take more drugs. After three days I was allowed to have my clothes back, which was a relief.

There was so much human suffering at Rozelle. No one seemed to care about the patients—most of the nurses reminded me of Melanie. I believe they enjoyed the power and control over those in their care. I didn't really get to know any of the patients. I was busy trying to plot my escape, but everywhere I went I was watched. Then I decided I would ask to sit outside in the garden. A nurse followed a group of us and we all sat down. After about an hour, I seized my chance to make a run for it. I ran as fast as I could around the front of the building and dived under a parked car. Within minutes the orderlies came running out to look for me. They ran straight past the car and then went inside. I knew they would call the police, so

I ran into someone's backyard and hid there until it grew dark.

I had escaped, but I was wanted for two armed robberies and escaping from custody, and I was a suicide risk. I wanted to find John, so I called Long Bay Prison. They told me he had been admitted to the Prince Henry Hospital and was recovering from a stroke. I then called the hospital and was able to speak to John, who told me to come and visit him. I knew the police would be looking for me, so I would have to be careful. Next morning I made my way to the Prince Henry Hospital. He told me he was faking his illness, and had fooled the doctors. He said that a friend had taken our car from where Torry had parked it at Artarmon and driven it to the carpark of the motel in Chatswood where we had stayed before. The guns were still stashed in the boot. John told me he didn't have any clothes— they had been taken away so that he couldn't escape. I kissed him and went for a walk around the hospital.

In one room I saw an old patient who looked about John's size. I waited until he went to sleep, then pinched his clothes and took them to John's room. John told me to meet him outside on the main road and to have a taxi waiting. I dialled a cab from a phone box. When John appeared he looked quite a sight in the borrowed clothes, but I was just terribly relieved to have him back. We took the taxi to his friend Jill's place in Mascot and she paid the fare. John borrowed some money from her, and then we went off to find our beloved car.

When we got to the Chatswood motel we discovered that the car had been broken into. John cursed the thieves and vowed revenge. I didn't care too much—it was good the car was there at all. To John's amazement the guns were still hidden safely in the boot. We filled up with petrol, then John decided to head off to the lights of Kings Cross.

"Okay, I want you to roll a couple of guys," he ordered. "When ya through we're heading off." "But the cops are after us," I objected.

"If you want these tablets," he told me, showing me a bottle of Valium, "you'll do as I say."

I asked him if I could have a knife to protect myself with—it was so dangerous here. He handed me a small gun and some ammunition. "Don't get busted," he said. "I'll be watching you."

I walked to the El Alamein Fountain, right in the centre of the Cross. Heaps of working girls were standing around waiting for a trick. Most of them looked to be strung out on some mind-altering drug. As I stood there a few drunks approached me and I told them to rack off. Then two policemen walked towards me.

"Aren't you the same girl we saw here a while back?" the older one said.

I knew I had been recognised and because I was carrying a gun I made a run for it.

"Hey, stop, Roxanne, we're not going to hurt you," the cop told me. They knew I was a problem kid, but they didn't know I had a gun on me, as well as plenty of extra bullets. Within seconds they had me on the ground. "Okay, don't do anything silly," I was told. "We're going to take you to the station for questioning."

Sitting in Kings Cross police station was a nightmare. Where was John? Why hadn't he helped me? I asked the sergeant on duty if I could visit the toilet, where I dumped the gun. I was never caught for that. The police arranged for me to go to a youth hostel in the Cross. Then the police called the Child Protection Unit and discovered I was a runaway. So they made another call to the Department of Youth and Community Services, because they thought I was a child at risk. Finally arrangements were made to have me admitted to Minda, a locked institution for juvenile offenders.

minda and mulawa

⁐

I arrived at Minda vowing that I'd never let them take control over me. I was thrown into a Time-out cell within minutes, then restrained, stripped and submitted to a medical exam. I knew what I had to do. I screamed out for the staff to let me call my dad. Eventually they agreed to this, and I left a message with Jill at Mascot. I told her where I was and said they wouldn't let me out because I was on remand for two armed robberies. So unless John came to Minda I wouldn't be able to see him.

After this I sat in the cell slashing my wrist. The same old self-destructive pathway. As I watched the blood pour out I felt a release of the stress inside me. One of the youth workers looked through the little plastic window of my cell. "Jesus, she's bleeding!" he yelled. They let me out and took me to a medical room where I had stitches put in my arm yet again. The nurse wrapped a bandage around my wrist and I told her that if I was put back in the cell I would hang myself. I don't think I really would have. I was just scared of being trapped in that little room.

As the nurse discussed the situation with another youth worker, the doorbell rang and I heard a familiar voice. "I've come to visit Roxanne Darton." It was John. I could see the shadow of another man behind him—he had brought someone with him.

"Dad!" I screamed.

"I'm sorry, Mr Darton, but Roxanne is not allowed any visitors at the moment," the nurse told him.

Then came the shock. John pulled out a rifle and aimed it at the nurse's head. "Let her out or I'll blow ya fuckin' head off!" he shouted.

Quickly the youth worker slammed shut the steel safety door and called the police. But I was so thankful John had come—I knew he wouldn't let me down. The Lidcombe police arrived and searched the grounds for John and his companion. There was no sign of them.

After this incident Susan, one of the Welfare workers, talked to me. "Do you understand why you are here in Minda, Roxanne?" she asked.

"Don't talk to me!" I screamed. "You wouldn't let me see my dad. Next time he'll use his gun."

"Your father is a menace, Roxanne," she told me. "You have been placed here for care and protection and you have two charges of armed robbery against you. I suggest you accept the fact that you are in Minda."

I would never accept it. We were sitting opposite two large windows. I stood up, picked up a chair and smashed them both. The youth workers restrained me. They held my hands behind my back and threw me into the Time-out room. I heard one of the staff say: "What are we going to do with this one?"

I stayed in Minda for three weeks on remand. Then it was time for me to appear again before Rod Blackmore at Bidura Children's Court. During those three weeks I was given sedatives every day, and every day I slashed my arms. Once again I was given a bodyguard. Minda was a typical Welfare locked institution. Each child had a room, there was a main television lounge and two schoolrooms. Being so drugged-out, I wasn't really capable of writing—the teacher gave me colouring books instead. I got so bored that I would smash things. I enjoyed being destructive. I felt people took notice of me.

I recall one day in the schoolroom when the teacher was ignoring me and paying attention to another girl. I picked up a small table and threw it through a window, then pushed the alarm buttons. Every day I destroyed things, and afterwards I would begin to destroy myself, cutting my arms.

One morning Sue told me I was due to appear in court the next day. "I want to make a phone call," I said. They thought it might help to calm me down. I was led into the reception area, where I dialled John's number. As the phone rang I prayed that he would answer.

A voice came on the line. "Jill speaking."

"Is John there?"

"Yeah, wait on."

"Hurry up, Roxanne," the youth worker told me.

Then I heard his voice. "John, it's me. I'm going to Bidura Court tomorrow. Please be there."

Suddenly the line went dead. The Minda staff had been listening on another line and realised who I was talking to. "Fuck you!" I shouted. I ripped the telephone wire right out of the wall, then smashed the instrument. Wayne, one of the youth workers, grabbed me by the hair and threw me into Time-out. I screamed uncontrollably until three in the morning, then passed out.

I woke to find I had blood all over me. Then I remembered that I had slashed my wrist. I was cleaned up and given another injection. Later that morning I was driven to Bidura Court where I was separated from the other kids. The court hadn't got over my previous appearance there, and they tried to keep me calm by giving me one cigarette after another.

"Hey, why is she allowed to smoke but we're not?" shouted one of the kids. A youth worker's response was to come up and take my cigarette off me. "Fuck you!" I yelled and kicked at the bars holding me in. The workers decided they would fetch a counsellor to talk to me. They were very nervous about my history of self-mutilation and thought I would eventually succeed in killing myself. A middle-aged woman came and sat down beside me. I told her to fuck off and said no one would ever be able to work me out except John, my dad.

I don't know what happened to John, he never showed up. I was called into court and escorted before the magistrate. Mr Blackmore said I was a very disturbed young lady and that I needed to be incarcerated for my own protection. I told him that if they hadn't locked me up I wouldn't have gone off my brain. He consulted a few reports and ordered that I undergo psychological evaluation in Minda.

I then returned to Minda and was given more drugs. I'd been given so many drugs throughout my life that I'd forgotten what it was like to be free of them.

There were a few really pleasant youth workers in Minda.

I became very attached to one of them—Sarah. When she was on duty I felt myself slowly allowing her to get close to me. She would hold my hand—she made me feel human. I wasn't used to affection, in fact I don't think I'd ever been held by another woman like that. Sarah was like a mother to me and whenever she was on duty I would cling to her like a baby.

But even though I had Sarah for about one per cent of the time, things as a whole did not improve for me in Minda. Most of my days were spent either in isolation or being stitched up. The nurse, Tanya, was really nice. I certainly kept her in a job. One day while I was in the surgery I picked up a bottle of pills and refused to give them back. Tanya told the youth worker waiting outside the door and he dragged me out to the reception area. They told me I was a little shit and would never be allowed in the surgery again. Tanya came out looking angry and told me I was very bad. I felt rejected. One of the kids had left a baseball bat in the reception area, and I picked it up and smashed all the windows. The workers were too scared to touch me—they waited until I'd finished then dragged me to Time-out. I was held down, stripped, then given a nightie and the inevitable injection. I stayed there two days, scratching at myself, crying and praying to God to change my life so that someone would love me and want me. After lunch on the second day two workers, a male and a female, came in and ordered me to get dressed.

"Right, Roxanne," the male youth worker said, and signalled for me to follow them. I was led outside to a waiting car.

"Where are we going?" I asked. "Shut up," was the response.

About half an hour later we drove through a gateway and I saw the sign. We had reached my next nightmare: Mulawa Women's Prison. I couldn't believe that Minda was sending me, a juvenile, to Mulawa. Two officers led me inside, questioned me and handed me a green tracksuit. Then I was taken into a shower area and told to strip. When I refused the officers held me down and forcibly started to remove my clothes. "Okay, I'll do it," I told them. I always hated having showers because of what John used to do to me, but now I had no choice. I shook and felt my heart beating in fear as the hot water hit my body.

One of the screws asked me about all the scars on my arms. I told her I hated myself. This convinced them I was mad, and I was committed to the psychiatric ward of the prison, which was named Rose Scott. It was horrific. There were about six steel cells, and I was told I would have to stay in my cell until the other inmates voted whether I should be allowed out or not. I couldn't handle being locked up there and was frightened I would have a panic attack. I asked if I could see a doctor, but was told to shut up.

"Please don't lock me in!" I screamed. I was freaking out in that small space. I begged them to open the door. I needed air. I felt claustrophobic. Another prisoner walking past had a packet of smokes in her hand. "Hey, can I have a cigarette?" I begged. She pushed three smokes and a box of matches through the air vent and I sat on my bed puffing away. I looked at the graffiti on the cell wall. Someone had scrawled: *A good screw is hard to find*. How true, I thought.

Three hours later I renewed my pleas to be let out, but the screws didn't care. So I lit a match and set fire to the mattress and blanket. Within minutes my cell was ablaze. I didn't care, I couldn't breathe anyway. The fear inside me of being trapped was so strong that the fire seemed irrelevant. As smoke filled the room outside one of the prisoners alerted the screws, who came running in with a fire hose. They squirted the mattress and blanket and left me sopping wet. I curled up into a ball and closed my eyes.

Next day I was let out of my cage after lunch. Rose Scott didn't seem like a proper psychiatric wing at all. A psychiatrist visited only once a week, so the inmates were lucky to get to see him. The doctor didn't really seem to care about them or even listen to them properly. They were simply kept on drugs. The only form of entertainment was a large television set.

A week later I was transferred to the dormitory, where I was given a bed between two murderers. One was pregnant, the other was crazy. One afternoon I had a severe panic attack. I hyperventilated into a fit and passed out. The screw accused me of faking it. They didn't understand anything about my problems, they just left me lying on the bed. I recovered, but I was terrified I would have another attack—I knew I would receive no help. In the end they did give me some Valium that day, but never offered me any therapy.

After lunch I asked one of the screws if I could call my lawyer. I had been assigned a Sydney solicitor. He was shocked to hear that I had been sent to Mulawa and that I had slashed my wrists. He told me that he would get me out of there. Within two hours the screws came to get me, and told me I was leaving. I was taken back to Minda. The staff there did not celebrate my return. I received a big lecture and some pills.

Although I'd hated Mulawa, I think I hated Minda more. I was sent into the boys' section, put in a cell without a blanket and left to freeze. As they escorted me to the cell I asked what I had done wrong. They told me none of the workers wanted to work with me and that I had to be isolated. Once again I was punished for being me. I kicked at the door, screamed and begged to be let out. All I wanted was to be treated the same as the other kids.

I passed two days sitting in that lonely cell. I thought about my mother and wondered where my father was living now. Why was life so painful? I felt so alone, with just a cock roach or two to keep me company. That night I wet the bed.

The staff at Minda were threatening to go out on strike because of me, and they were supported by their union. The problem was that there there was nowhere else for me to go. The psychiatrists declared I was not mad, while all the Welfare workers said I was too bad to cope with. There was now only one day to go before my next appearance at Bidura, and while I waited I was kept caged like an animal. That night, however, Sarah came to visit me. She gave me a cigarette, my pills and a hot drink.

I woke early next day and was given an injection to keep me calm. Sometimes I wondered why I was kept so drugged. Although the drugs were supposed to have a calming effect, I felt they also stirred my anger. I was so stoned most of the time that my mind was in a fog and I lost my will to care what happened.

Mr Blackmore, the magistrate, was in Court One at Bidura. As I entered I saw that Lisa Bennett, the Young Offenders Support Manager, was also present. The charges against me were read out and the hearing began. After listening to the evidence, Mr Blackmore decided to adjourn the case until after lunch. Although I didn't realise it at the time, the whole of the New South Wales Department of Youth and Community Service was now on the verge of going out on strike because of me. They said the strike action would continue until I was removed from Minda. No one wanted me. I couldn't believe I was so bad—there were murderers in Minda, after all. Why had they chosen to strike over me?

During the lunch break Elizabeth Davies visited me and told me I might have to be sent back to Mulawa. There was no alternative. I cried and begged not to be sent back there. In the end Mr Blackmore decided to remand me back to Minda for another two weeks. I gained a reprieve, even if the staff did not agree with it.

At Minda, the staff tried desperately to keep me in a routine during those two weeks. For most of the time they allowed me to go into the classroom with my bodyguard, because the law stated that all children had to attend school. During one of the lessons a man walked in. He told us he was a film maker and that he was doing research for a new film, "Turbo Kids". He was tall and blond and introduced himself as James Ricketson. I did not realise how important he would become in my life.

James talked to some of the kids. He wanted to hear our stories and find out what street kids were all about, how they lived. I still had stitches in my arms and both my wrists were bandaged. James asked one of the youth workers about me. I liked James instinctively. I felt he really understood children— otherwise why should he waste his time coming out to Minda?

James told me he had a five-year-old son, Jesse. He asked me about my life and I told him all about my childhood. I knew he was really listening to me. We spent a few hours talking together, and afterwards I wrote him a letter.

Dear James,

Thank you for coming to see us kids. You are really nice,
thank you for talking to me. I never had a father, all my
life I wished that I had a dad like you, I know you cared.
I wish you would talk to me again. Sometimes I do really
stupid things and I want to die but I believe I still have a
little spark left in me, I want to be good. Please help me
change my life, I know I can. I've never asked anyone for
help in my life ... please help me ...

Love, Roxanne

James came back a few times and even brought Jesse
with him. He was—he is—a wonderful human being. I felt a
strong connection to this forty-year-old film-maker. Sarah told
me that my behaviour was different when he came to Minda
during those two weeks. Eventually he finished his research,
and for me it was back to the subnormal.

Inevitably, the head staff member realised that Sarah was
getting too close to me, so they took her away and gave me a
guard called Elizabeth instead. I hated her the moment I first
saw her. She picked on me, stirred me, disliked me intensely—
-the feeling was mutual. She reminded me of a youth worker
at Nyandi who used to send me into isolation just to punish
me mentally. Elizabeth was about thirty. She had long blonde
hair. One day she told me I mustn't talk to one of the boys.
When I asked why, she told me that she made the rules. At that
moment she reminded me of my mother. I grabbed her long
hair and started biting and punching her. I never understood
why I used to lash out, I really think the pills exacerbated
my anger. Elizabeth decided to charge me with assault, and
I didn't really blame her for that. I suppose I'd taken it upon
myself to use her as my emotional punching-bag.

Within seconds of the attack I was grabbed by two male
youth workers and driven to Lidcombe police station. All the

way I screamed out: "I hate you, I hate you!" I thought about James and wished that he would adopt me. I knew this was a fantasy, that it could never happen. I envied Jesse his great dad. I had nothing. The police didn't even bother to type a confession; the staff told them I was uncontrollable, and maybe they thought I might start smashing up the station. Instead they came to interview me at Minda. They gave me a good talking-to and told me to try to be a good girl, otherwise I would end up in the big house, the prison. They didn't realise I'd already been there.

The next morning a guy called Mark came into my isolation cell. The staff figured a male bodyguard would be better for me. For once they were right. Mark told me I had to stay in isolation until the staff decided what they would do about me. I lay down on the floor and began to cry. I hadn't had a good cry for a long time. I sobbed that I wanted to be good, I just didn't know how to start. Mark came over and put his arm around me, then gave me a glass of milk, some toast—and more pills.

A female youth worker brought in a book for him to read to me, and as I lay there and listened, for once the tears flowed instead of blood. I don't think any youth workers besides Mark and Sarah had shown me affection before and I loved it. For a short while I felt like I was a little girl again. Mark was a really caring person, but the Welfare system was always looking out to make sure no one got too close to those in its charge.

Meanwhile, the strike situation reached crisis point. The Welfare workers decided they would definitely all go out on strike unless I was removed from Minda within two hours. I was told to get dressed and was driven back to Bidura Children's Court.

"Roxanne Darton, you have been charged with insubordination and assault. Do you understand what that means?" As the youth worker waited for my reply I kicked the microphone. "Go fuck yourself! I hate you!" I screamed.

Rod Blackmore, the magistrate, asked my case manager, Lisa Bennett, what psychological tests I'd had. The strike issue of the New South Wales youth workers was also discussed.

Lisa Bennett had contacted James to see whether he could come up with any answers. As I waited in the cell at Bidura, Lisa and james came in to see me.

"Roxanne," Lisa said, "this is a really serious situation. We have no idea where to place you because you are still on remand on some grave charges. The court is not prepared to grant you bail. We also have the strike problem—the Minda staff have voted to go out on strike because they cannot handle you. There really does not seem to be any other option than Mulawa."

I told them there was no way in this world I was going back there. I said I'd rather be dead. Then I sobbed out: "James, please let me come and live with you. You said you would help me!" I held on to him and began to cry.

Lisa and James drafted a letter to present to Rod Blackmore. He also obtained statements from women friends of James's who supported him and offered to help. Then it was time for me to go before the bench again. As I waited for my fate to be determined, I prayed hard.

Mr Blackmore expressed concern that James was a single father, and that I was a child victim of sexual abuse. But in view of the crisis situation with the threatened strike action, he recommended that I be placed in the daily custody of Mr James Ricketson of Palm Beach, except for weekends, for a certain number of weeks, after which I would be transferred to his care full-time. (I was to return to Minda at weekends for the time being.) I was overjoyed. But as I stood there in court, I wondered why no one had bothered to find out my true identity. I hated lying. I really wanted to tell James that I was not Roxanne Lee Darton, aged seventeen, I was Elizabeth Lee, twenty-one, a drug addict and a runaway from Western

Australia wanted in three states. I knew inside me that it was time to tell the truth...but not just yet.

I told James he was the nicest man I had ever met. Everyone else I had ever encountered had always used me in some way. James wanted nothing in return, just the satisfaction of helping me. I realised how lucky I was. I vowed to stop slashing my arms, taking pills and behaving like an animal. I vowed to erase John's influence out of my life.

As I walked out of the court that day I was besieged by reporters who handed me their cards and asked if I would go on television to tell my side of the story about the Minda strike, which was big news. There was a lot of press coverage. One reporter was from Channel Nine: he represented the program *A Current Affair*. Then I was driven back to Minda, where I was released into .James's care. As we walked to his car, a blue mini-van, I wondered where my life was heading now.

palm beach-and canberra

∽

We drove out of the city, over the Harbour Bridge on to the North Shore, and took the road for the peninsula and Palm Beach. Once we reached Narrabeen, I began to notice how beautiful the houses were. James told me that a lot of wealthy people lived in this area. He said that although his house was quite modest, it had a million-dollar view. He explained that he was just a struggling writer and film-maker and warned me not to expect too much.

Palm Beach was lovely. James stopped at a small corner store and asked me if I wanted anything. "I need some corks-er, tampons, I mean," I replied. He looked at me the way any concerned father would. "Righto," he said and went into the shop. I think he may have felt a bit embarrassed. He came out again with seven different packets.

James was right, his house was no mansion. It was an old, rundown weatherboard house perched on the cliff-top, and it certainly had a magnificent view. As we sat inside sipping tea, I told James I wanted to thank him for believing in me.

It seemed really strange being alone in a house with a single man and his son. I had lived in institutions (and in a car) for so long. The first few days were really good, but I did find it hard to settle in properly. I called Torry, and he said he would come to visit. In fact he turned up the very next day. He wasn't happy and told me that he wanted to get away from everything. I was feeling very nervous that day, because next morning I was due back at Bidura Court to face the charges of armed robbery and malicious damage. Even though James was so kind, I didn't feel my new situation could last too long. I didn't feel as though Palm Beach was my sort of area. I felt no one here would accept me—after all, why would anyone want a drug-addicted criminal living in their midst?

Torry and I decided there was only one thing to do. He suggested we skip the state and head for Canberra. Once I ran away from James we knew the police would be looking for us—and we were both considered suicide risks. Looking back, I think that Torry and I together were like a nuclear bomb ready to explode.

We left James's house and stole a car that looked like an old ambulance. Torry drove it for about half an hour, then we discovered we had lost one wheel. No joke—that car was running on three wheels. We slammed on the brakes and decided the vehicle was a fate worse than death. I told Torry I didn't mind hitch-hiking so long as he was with me. Most of the time I was off my face anyway, thanks to the drugs, so I wasn't really that scared.

It didn't take long before a guy who looked to be in his forties picked us up in his Kombi van. He seemed a bit weird to begin with, but turned out to be quite harmless, and even ended up buying us lunch. Eventually we arrived in Canberra. It had only taken three and a half hours, and we were now in the Australian Capital Territory.

I think a small part of Torry longed to be normal. Like any tourist, he wanted to visit Parliament House. But I had other ideas. "Come on, Torry, I need some pills," I told him. We broke into a chemist's, stole a ton of Valium, then decided to get smashed.

Canberra is probably a great city if you are a rich fifty year-old—but it had absolutely nothing to offer a pair of wayward street kids. By now it was beginning to get dark, and we decided to have some fun. We found a late-night chemist's that also sold toys, and pinched two cap-guns and a reel of caps. Across the street we saw the police head quarters. "Come on, Torry," I said. We went into the grounds surrounding the building and found the perfect spot, right under the window of a senior officer who was at his desk.

"Right, Torry, when I say run—you RUN!" I shouted. We let off a couple of rounds and within seconds about twenty cops had jumped out in all directions, thinking a madman was on the loose. "RUN, Torry!" I yelled, but they grabbed us and gave us a real talking-to.

"Take your firecrackers somewhere else, you little smart-arses," a sergeant said. "If I see you hanging around again you'll be arrested it. Got it?" He gave us a stern look and sent us on our way.

It was getting late by now, and it was very cold. Torry and I wondered where we should spend the night. I told him I wanted to go back to James's house. He told me to forget about James. We found a telephone box and looked in the phone book for a youth refuge. We found two, so we made a couple of calls. The lady at the Downer Refuge told me to catch a cab there and said she would pay the fare. When we arrived I thought it looked pretty good for a refuge, it was a modern, clean place. We knocked on the door and a youth worker let us in.

"I'm Val," she told me, and looked at Torry. "I'm sorry, but he can't stay here, this is an all-girls refuge. I assumed you were both girls when you mentioned the name Tony on the phone."

I told her there was no way I was going to be separated from Torry.

"Give me your full names and I'll make a few calls and see what we can do," Val said. As we waited outside the office door we realised she was talking to the police, checking to see if we were runaways. We couldn't get out of the front door because it had a double lock, designed to keep outsiders from coming in and the girls from getting out. We panicked. We knew the cops would soon be on their way, so I picked up a chair and threw it through a window. "Run!" I screamed, and we fled.

We ran and ran until we reached the city centre, where we stopped outside a building site with scaffolding fifteen storeys high. Here Torry and I made a pact. We would take all the pills we had, then jump off the top. I swallowed about thirty sleeping pills and a handful of Normison as well. Slowly we began to climb. I grew drowsier by the minute and almost fell a few times. What saved me was the fact that each storey had planks for the workmen to stand on. We were almost halfway up and I had stopped for a rest when we heard sirens. Uniformed police, the Rescue Squad and ambulance men arrived and began to climb the scaffolding ready to grab us. We never got a chance to jump—as I went on climbing, a copper seized hold of Torry.

"Rox, stop, please don't jump!" Torry screamed out.

Part of me wanted to jump but I knew that I would be leaving behind the only person who really cared about me. Anyway, as I reached for the next rung, a rescue cop grabbed me and pulled me down to ground level. I bit him and punched him. "Sweetheart, what were you doing up there?" he asked me. "You could have been killed." By way of reply I showed him the slash marks on my arm and told him to get a real job.

We were taken to the police station, where the cops decided I needed help. I was sick of hearing people tell me this. I knew I was messed up. I wanted to live on drugs. I wanted to block out my pain and to treat society the way it had treated me. I was on a merry-go-round spinning out of control.

The police took me to Woden Valley Hospital. I was barely awake, but remember being dragged into Casualty. "Where's Torry?" I asked groggily. "I'm not staying here. Call James." I tried to make a run for it, but the cops seized hold of me. Suddenly I grabbed one of the copper's guns out of its holster.

I had my finger on the trigger. Then the other cop pulled his gun on me and warned me to put it down. Two nurses dived for cover; the Casualty department emptied. My brain was swimming in a deep fog. I wouldn't have hurt the cop. I never had any intention of hurting anyone. I just wanted to get out of the hospital. I felt trapped and couldn't stand the thought that I was about to have my stomach pumped out and my drugs taken away. Being stoned provided me with a security blanket that covered my fears and suppressed my emotions.

As the cop with the gun threatened to blow my head off I made my decision. I still had a little faith that someday I might succeed in changing my life. Slowly I put down the weapon and everyone breathed heavy sighs of relief. After that the doctors put me to bed, gave me a police guard and let me sleep off the drugs.

I woke next morning thinking it had all been a bad dream, only to find a huge cop standing next to my bed. He told me it was time for me to be a good girl and start getting better.

"Go fuck yourself! I hate you. You're a bunch of losers—get out of my life!" I yelled.

"Just calm down, Roxanne. Here's your breakfast, so eat up. It'll do you good."

"Stop telling me what to do. You're not my father. I want to call James," I said.

But the cop refused to let me do this, so I picked up the breakfast tray and threw it. I tried to run, but I was too weak. My legs got me outside the door and then I collapsed.

After this the Canberra police decided that the psychiatric unit at Woden Valley Hospital wasn't the right place for me. Because I was a suicide risk and a danger to myself they had me transferred to a locked children's home called Quamby. The police didn't treat me too badly, considering all the stress I'd put them through. They escorted me to Quamby that same day. It was no different to all the other lock-ups I'd been to. As soon as

I stepped inside I was given the drill: strip, squat for medical examination, then shower. I didn't feel like any arguments so I just followed orders. I wondered what James was thinking. I hoped he knew how sorry I was to have run away. All my life people had told me that I had made a lot of mistakes. I liked to think of them as "learning experiences." As I stood under the shower I tried really hard to think of a time when I was truly happy. I couldn't... Suddenly I was jerked back to reality when the youth worker pointed to my hair, saying: "Wash that lot properly too."

I didn't like Quamby at all. I felt alienated the very first day, when I was told not to talk to the other kids. I slept in an isolation cell and ate alone. A youth worker called Mary brought me my dinner that night and told me she was to be my cover for the night. So I was to have a twenty-four hour bodyguard once again.

My reaction was predictable. I smashed my plate and slashed my arm. My poor arms were so mutilated it wasn't funny. Yet I didn't want to die. I was simply very, very angry. As the blood ran down my wrist I asked Mary why I was the only one who had to have a guard. I begged her for equal treatment. The nurse came to bandage me up and I was given two Normison tablets to help me to sleep—I was used to far more than that, and they ended up tripling the dose. I was put into bed and Mary watched me all night.

After five days in Quamby the staff decided they were unable to control me because I was so violent and my mood swings were completely unpredictable. They threatened action if I wasn't removed. No matter where I went, every welfare department agreed on one thing: they had never experienced any girl as traumatised as I was.

Next day I was taken by police van to Belconnen Prison. I was led into a small cell and once more told to strip. A prison warder in a blue uniform appeared and I was held down and given another injection. The Belconnen prison staff left me in solitary confinement for three days to withdraw from drugs, then I was integrated into the rest of the prison population. This was the first prison I'd been to that had male and female prisoners together.

"Good day," one of the male prisoners greeted me. "Wanna game?" He offered me a pool cue, but I refused. I had decided the best thing was to keep to myself.

Finally some good news arrived—a letter from James. He explained that after I left he had wondered where I'd gone and was surprised to learn I was in Canberra. He told me he loved me and would continue to help me. I was surprised he could still believe in me. Maybe there was a faint glimmer of hope.

That afternoon Dr Una Freestone, a child psychologist from the ACT Child and Adolescent Unit, came to see me. All through my life I had seen so many therapists. I treated each one to a game and tried my best to destroy the power I believed they held over me. Una Freestone was different. She really listened to me, and when I realised this I opened up my feelings to her and began to tell her the story of my life. As I talked, tears filled my eyes. Not tears of self-pity... rather of anger against myself. I felt as though I deserved to be treated badly. We talked for almost two hours. It was the first time I had allowed any therapist to get close to me. Dr Freestone told me I had a personality disorder and said that I need good, positive experiences. Since I'd never had any, I didn't understand how important they were.

After a week in Belconnen I was released to a refuge in Canberra. It was run by a group of lesbians. Within minutes of arriving one of the older women started making eyes at me. I picked up the phone and called James, asking him to please come and get me NOW. He really is my guardian angel. He drove down to Canberra at once and came straight to the refuge.

He ended up having to threaten the hostel workers to release me-I'm sure they'd had other plans for me. Then James and I visited the Canberra Art Gallery. It was really impressive. I have to confess that as we sat over cappucinos in the cafe, I was contemplating how I could pinch one of the masterpieces to present to James.

After my Canberra escapade, Minda did not want me back even at weekends. James talked to me very seriously and we decided that if I ever felt like running away again, I was to tell him. He always supported me. He talked to me every day, took photos of me and kept a detailed diary. His son, young Jesse, became my brother and my friend. I loved living in this family unit. But sometimes it wasn't easy—I had never lived in such a secure environment before, and although I loved James, I still didn't feel safe. Every day I still showered fully dressed, and at night I'd stay awake in bed as long as I could. I had a big fear that James might want more than just to love me as a daughter. On top of this, I had this big drug dependency problem.

That first week back at Palm Beach the Department of Youth and Community Services assigned me a case-worker called Sharon Lennon. Her job was to check on me and make sure everything was all right. I didn't see her very often. Most of the time I was left to my own devices.

Throughout all my time at Palm Beach, I still heard from John. Although he was away on the other side of the harbour, he still made it very clear he intended to have me back. He would call and threaten me and even had people follow me to James's house.

James decided it would be a good idea to enrol in school. I agreed, and chose Barrenjoey High School, nearby on the peninsula. Even though I attended only half a day, five times a week, I loved it. Suddenly I was making new friends. When my birthday came round, James said I could invite a few of them over. I ended up with two hundred drunken teenagers, neigh-bours' complaints and the arrival of the Mona Vale police.

After the Canberra fiasco I received three telephone calls: one from John, another from my girlfriend Norma Bateson, and the third from Torry, who was now at home in Wollongong. I asked Torry to come and see me, but he sounded unsure. He said that if he skipped bail his mum would lose her house, which she had nominated as surety. However, he said he would try to come. After Norma rang I asked James if she could visit for the weekend. Norma was sixteen, and I had met her in Minda. She had been abused as a child and couldn't live at home. As it happened, Norma, a friend from school called Justin and Torry all turned up at the same time. Justin was only sixteen, but his mother allowed him to borrow her car sometimes. That weekend we all decided to borrow the car. "Come on, you guys," Justin urged us, "let's have some fun."

I had swallowed some Valium pills and drunk a few scotch and-cokes—Tarry had brought a bottle ofbourbon with him. "I don't want to get into any trouble," I told the others.

"Oh, come on, Roxie," Norma said.

Soon I found myself being talked into another armed robbery. I was pretty stoned, and slowly the idea seemed to become attractive. We decided the best place to rob would be a chemist's—our main purpose was to find drugs and cash. The boys wanted the cash and Norma and I wanted the drugs.

We took Justin's mother's car, a Holden Commodore, and drove down to Narrabeen, where we spotted an all-night chemist. Torry and I walked in, and even though we were not armed, we told the guy behind the counter it was a stick-up. He didn't realise we had no weapon. Within seconds he hit the alarm and made contact with the police. We took off at high speed, driving at almost 100 kilometres an hour up Barren-joey Road. At North Avalon, Justin said he had to phone his mum, so we pulled up at a telephone box. Two minutes later, an off-duty police officer from Mona Vale station had us under arrest.

We were conveyed to Mona Vale police station where we were charged, finger-printed and photographed. We were all bailed to appear at Bidura Children's Court a month later. James wasn't at all impressed with our behaviour, and neither were the police. While I was in custody I slashed my wrist and a doctor had to be called. Once again I thought I had succeeded in destroying the faith of the only human being who really cared about me. But once again James stood by me.

He told me he thought it would be a good idea if I made some other friends, and encouraged me to join the Youth Theatre at Narrabeen. He said that maybe I needed a new and different release for my emotions other than slashing my wrists—perhaps drama was the answer.

I took the bus to the Youth Theatre and arrived feeling quite scared as I walked inside. I was introduced to a group of young people, most of them nice little North Shore kids who'd been pampered from day one. I didn't stay very long—it wasn't a very successful outing, my first day at the Theatre.

When I got home I was told that a police officer from Mona Vale was waiting to question me about a police radio I was supposed to have stolen. The officer, who was off-duty, told James that he thought a quiet chat with me would be the best thing. His name was Martin and he took me down to Palm Beach, where he tried to assault me. I managed to get home safely, thanks to James, but that little interlude scared me.

I knew the police at Mona Vale disliked me and the feeling was mutual. Now I knew how corrupt a police officer could be. I was pretty appalled when James told me next day that he was very worried about my behaviour, and thought that it might be best if I went into custody at Mona Vale station overnight for my own protection. I was due to appear in court the next day on the charges of armed robbery.

When I heard James telephone the police, I grabbed my bag and two hundred dollars from his wallet. I knew the cops would be there soon, so I bolted. I swallowed a handful of pills and then jumped out of my bedroom window. I ran down to Palm Beach, dialled a cab and waited. It soon arrived.

"Where to?" bellowed the driver.

"Sydney International Airport," I mumbled. The drive took forty-five minutes.

At the airport I walked up to the Qantas counter. "One ticket to anywhere on the next available flight," I said.

The attendant looked at me as if I'd come from another planet. "Do you have a passport?" she asked.

I shook my head.

"Then there's only one flight you can take. To Auckland. You don't need a passport to get to New Zealand."

new zealand

❧

September, 1987: as the plane touched down on the runway at Auckland Airport, my head was still up in the clouds. I don't remember the flight, nor how I got to a hotel in Mangarie, but someone must have helped me. When I awoke next morning the television in my room was on full-blast. "Kiwi kids are Weetbix kids!" the commercial belted out. *What do they mean, Kiwi kids*, I thought. *Why not Aussie kids*? Then I realised where I was.

Had I gone mad? I was in a strange country, wanted by the Australian police, I had no money and didn't know a soul. My hotel bill would use up my last few dollars. There was a knock at the door. "Room service," a voice said. A man who I took to be Maori brought in a breakfast tray. I decided to ask him if there were any nearby youth hostels. He didn't know of any. We talked for a while, and finally he said: "You can stay at our place if you like." With some misgiving I agreed, wondering what I was letting myself in for.

Robert's family was actually from Samoa. From the outside their house looked quite normal, but inside it was a disaster. There were eleven people in the family, including Robert's grandparents, and they lived a traditional life. We all slept on straw mats and a great cooking pot simmered away ceaselessly. We ate stewed lamb night after night and the smell continually wafted through the house. I hadn't been there very long before

Hafa, the grandmother, summoned me to the kitchen and gave me an ultimatum. I had to marry Robert and sleep with him, otherwise they would throw me out on the street. I burst into tears, gathered up my clothing and walked out of the front door. Robert came running after me. "I don't want to marry you, just come back," he pleaded. I had nowhere else to go, so I went back. It was a great mistake. As soon as I entered the house again, Robert and his mother took me into a bedroom and beat me up.

I was told I could not leave the house unless Robert was with me. I was virtually a prisoner. I asked Tala, Robert's younger sister, why they were doing this to me. "Robert wants to take the family to live in Australia and gain Australian citizenship," she told me. I was their ticket to a brave new world. After the beating-up, I realised my medication was running low. I had a black eye and I thought my wrist might be fractured. I couldn't eat their food—the smell of the meat made me feel nauseous. I knew I had to escape, otherwise I'd be forced into a marriage I didn't want. I looked through my bag and discovered that Meli, Robert's mother, had taken my wallet and bank book. I was informed I would not get them back until I agreed to the marriage. She also told me that if I tried to escape she would call the Auckland police and tell them I was a wanted person. I had made another mistake and told them I was on the run—I thought it would put them off trying to force the marriage on me.

That evening, as darkness settled over Mangarie, I plotted my escape. I climbed out of a back window and found my way to a main road. I had no idea where I was. I hailed an approaching car. "I have to get to Wellington," I said.—"Yeah, all right, love, hop in," the driver responded. He was a Maori, in his forties, and seemed a little the worse for wear. I suspected he used needles. I told him how I'd been hijacked by a Samoan family and he invided me back to his flat in Auckland. I forgot about going to Wellington and gladly accepted his offer.

Ara was a salesman who lived from hand to mouth. He gave me a bed and provided me with meals for a few days, which I really appreciated. He made it clear I would have to leave by Friday because his mother was coming to visit him. He told me about Waikeke Island, which was about twenty minutes from Auckland by ferry and I decided to go there. After I left the flat I realised Ara had stolen my last ten dollars, but there was no way I was going back to his place in case someone from Robert's family spotted me.

I found the harbour and the main ferry terminal. There was a Russian cruise ship docked there, due to sail that day. I walked on board and went to the dining salon, where I had a wonderful meal, which I charged to one of the passenger's cabins. I thought of stowing away on the ship, but sense prevailed and I went over to the ferry terminal instead. The trip to Waiheke was pleasant, a cool breeze swept over me as we chugged along. Soon the island came in sight and I disembarked with a group of other passengers and headed to the beach. It was now late in the afternoon and I didn't have anywhere to sleep. I found a small corner store and bought a Coke with some loose change in my pocket, then went to the local park and swallowed a handful of pills.

As the sun went down the temperature dropped to eight degrees and I was frozen. I tried to keep walking, but the pills were putting me to sleep. I found a telephone box outside the park and called James, reversing the charges.

"Roxanne! Where are you?" he asked.

"New Zealand," I told him.

He almost dropped the phone. I told him I had come to Auckland to get away from the Mona Vale police. He told me to go to the nearest police station and get myself back to Australia. I said goodbye and then decided I wasn't ready to return to the comforts of Palm Beach. I picked up a rock and smashed the door of the phone box, then slowly sliced my wrist with a sliver of glass. I was such a failure. I was so angry at myself. I hated me.

Within half an hour I had passed out. I came to and found myself surrounded by police and medics. They bandaged my wrist, then took me back to Auckland in a police boat. I was taken to Auckland Base Hospital, where I had twenty-five stitches put in my wrist. The police were wary of me from the moment they set eyes on me, and I accepted that I was an extremely messed-up girl. They told me I was free to go once I left Casualty. I stood outside the hospital, wondering what to do next.

I went back to my former plan of going to Wellington and decided to hitch a ride on an early evening train. I chose a compartment occupied by a young woman and her small daughter. The woman asked me where I was going. I told her my story, and she told me hers. Her boyfriend had abused her and she was going to Wellington to try to find a women's refuge. Chrissie had long blonde hair and green eyes. Her daughter's name was Kate. Chrissie asked me if I wanted to hang out with her on the road, and I told her yes, a travelling companion would be great.

Chrissie had taken her boyfriend's Visa card. When we reached Wellington we decided we'd find a decent hotel. But first we walked around a shopping centre, thronged with late-night shoppers. Chrissie said she needed some new clothes and a suitcase for her stuff. We walked inside a posh-looking store. The shopkeeper was an Italian woman and she turned up her nose when she saw me. I was wearing a pair of scruffy leather pants and a red-and-white striped top. And I had a bandage on my wrist. "How can I help you?" she asked.

"Well," I said, looking around, "We'll take that leather case and one of those backpacks."

The bill came to $300 and she told me she would have to

call Visa for authorisation. As she dialled my heart pounded: were we about to get busted? I held my breath.

"Right," she said, "shall I wrap these for you?"

I grabbed our purchases and told her not to worry. We bolted.

There was no problem finding a hotel, and after we'd had hot showers, Kate announced she was hungry, so we went out to dinner. We ended up buying hot dogs and $500 worth of new clothes, courtesy of the boyfriend's Visa card, then headed back to the hotel. I called a doctor to our room, and he gave me a prescription for more Valium. There was an all-night chemist next to the hotel where I got my new supply.

When I returned to the hotel, Chrissie and I made plans to go to the South Island next morning, to Christchurch.

In the early hours of the morning we were woken by banging and shouting and our room was invaded by six uniformed cops. "Right, sweetheart, get your butt up," one of them told me. I was dragged out of bed, then made to sit in a chair with a flashlight shone into my eyes. Katie and Chrissie both cried— the cops felt sorry for them, but gave me the third degree. We were all taken to Wellington police station, then separated. I was taken to an interview room. The New Zealand cops were no different to the Australian ones—I hated them all. When they asked my age, I told the truth: I was fed up with lying. They asked me where my parents were, and I told them I had run away from my foster dad in Australia. The police then rang James and told him they had me in custody.

After this I was put into a freezing cell with not even a blanket. I'd hidden a razor blade in my shoe and started to cut my arms, then took half the Valium pills I had on me. Soon I was covered in blood.

'Jesus Christ!" one of the cops yelled out as he walked past.

My mind was so fogged-up that I couldn't understand what was happening. Three police officers opened the cell door and held me down, and a doctor arrived to stitch me up. "Get away from me! I hate you all! I want my dad. Please, let me go," I screamed. Eventually reality slapped me in the face. I was lying on my side, my hands handcuffed behind my back. Then two policewomen arrived, undid the handcuffs, and I was stripped except for my underpants and bra. They put a plastic space suit on me which zipped up the front, then I was handcuffed once more.

Two policemen sat outside my cell all night to make sure I didn't commit suicide. Next morning the doctor gave me another injection. I was denied bail-that was predictable and after a cup of warm milk and a some dry toast I was driven off to Poiriua Psychiatric Hospital.

Poiriua was a nightmare. It was a huge, cold, grey building surrounded by tall trees and a high fence. It could have come out of the Middle Ages. As the police led me inside I heard moans and groans—we walked past a row of steel cells and there were drugged bodies everywhere I looked. A male nurse led me to my room, where I was stripped and given a gown like a potato sack to wear. Then I was given the drill. If I played up, I would be put into the isolation room. The room I'd been allocated contained only a metal bed and steel chamber-pot. I was locked inside and left there overnight. Next day, another nurse took me for a shower. I was told that so long as I behaved myself I was allowed to talk to the other patients. This proved quite a feat. Cheryl was a schizophrenic who believed she had a direct line to God. Another man thought he was the Greek Prime Minister. And there were three old ladies with dementia. I was the youngest and sanest.

Eight metal cells ran along a hallway and the glare of the fluorescent lighting was enough to send anyone round the bend. Every meal time I had to sit with a woman who dribbled and spat and vomited up her food again. My cover nurse was called Jody: she followed me everywhere I went. I was given medication for the first few days, then take to see two psychologists. They knew I had a severe Valium addiction and thought the best treatment was to let me go through withdrawal in my cell.

During those days my mind was in a void. My skin poured out toxins while I shook and sweated. It was the hardest thing I'd ever experienced. I had been using Valium every day since I was thirteen. Finally, for the first time, I was drug free. After my withdrawal, I began to notice the most wonderful sounds. Birdsong, for instance. I hadn't realised how clear things could sound.

The staff at Poiriua treated me like dirt. The head nurse, Chris, took a particular dislike to me because I was Australian. Every time he was on duty he referred to me as "that Aussie piece of shit". After two weeks on remand I was transferred to the main section of the hospital. Here, although it was locked, the patients could walk around, watch television and do craft. Some were allowed to wear their own clothes, but not me. Then I met Raelene, a young Maori girl who suffered from schizophrenia. When she was on medication she was totally normal. I told Raelene I had to escape. I couldn't take it any longer. My anxiety was overwhelming.

Raelene had an idea. The craft room was locked, but it had a comparatively flimsy metal security door, and Raelene told me that with three other people she would be able to bend it. Since I had no clothes, after lunch she got me a white shirt and a black skirt, and I put these on beneath my hospital gown. I waited until the nurses were busy handing out medication, then managed to find three other patients who looked pretty strong. It took only a few seconds to break the door open and then I was free. I ran outside as fast as I could, across a field to the train station. The next train was due in five minutes, but I thought I spotted an ambulance in the distance and decided not to risk being caught on the platform. Back on the road I waved down a passing car. "Please, can you take me to Wellington?" I asked.

The driver, a middle-aged man, looked at me as though I was a weirdo. However, he gave me a lift as far as the next town, Lower Hutt. I walked around the streets then rested on a bench. Suddenly I heard a voice call: "Hey, you!" and saw two police officers coming towards me. I ran like hell.

I found my way to the carpark of the local hospital. I knew I would have to find a hiding-place because now, as well as being was an escapee and a suicide risk, I was also an illegal immigrant. I knew I needed help, and I figured that another psychiatric ward would be the perfect place. I walked into the casualty department. The nurse asked my name. "Tala," I told her. "I'm from Mangarie, in Auckland." When I saw the doctor I told her about my horrific panic attacks and my fear of being outside. She decided to admit me to the psych iatric ward and then gave me an injection of Valium. After three weeks of withdrawal I was back to being an addict. When she was called out of her room I stole a prescription pad and wrote myself a pill party.

Next morning I was seen by Grant, the hospital social worker. He was really caring. I told him how difficult my life had been, and how I couldn't stop mutilating myself. I had been cutting myself since I was thirteen. He was very understanding and seemed genuinely interested in me, so I opened up to him a little and asked him to help me find an answer to my problems.

Lower Hutt Hospital seemed a good place. I was put in a room with a sixteen-year-old girl who had anorexia nervosa. Grant visited me every day and spent a lot of time trying to help me. I began to feel as though he was my soul mate. During my second week in the hospital I was encouraged to paint. I loved art, it helped me to express myself. As I sat in the craft room one day, a nurse asked me if I would participate in a question-naire being conducted by a visiting psychologist. I agreed, and Grant led me to a room to meet the psychologist.

"Jesus Christ," I said to myself as he walked in. It was the same doctor I had seen at Poiriua. He seemed confused when he saw me. "But—aren't you Roxanne?" he asked me.—"No, my name is Tala," I told him. I waited until he was halfway through his questions, then said I needed to use the toilet.

I ran down the hallway and out of the hospital into a rose garden. Grant came running after me. "Roxanne!" he called out, "it's okay, please don't leave!" He caught up with me and I burst into tears. "I wanted to tell you the truth but I was too scared," I sobbed. Grant held me and told me everything would be okay, he said he would fight tooth and nail to keep me in the hospital. He didn't want me to go back to Poiriua. As we walked back to the ward he held my hand.

As I waited outside his office and overhead the phone call he was making, I became very nervous. I did what I'd always done in a panic situation—I ran. Grant gave chase, but I was too fast for him. I sat in a laneway pulling at my wrist and wondering why things always went wrong.

I managed to hitch a ride into Wellington, where I felt terribly alone. After three nights on the cold, windy streets I was at a complete loss. I didn't have the money to fly back to Australia. I thought about giving myself up to the police to stop the insane thoughts buzzing around my head. I realised my only real chance of getting help was to give myself up, and I made my way back to the Lower Hutt Hospital and walked through the casualty department. There were two police officers there, a male and a female, and they recognised me. The male officer seized hold of me. I struggled with him, managed to grab his cap, and ran. "Roxanne!" yelled the policewoman, "come back!" My heart was pumping in overdrive as I ran through the hospital gardens and hid in the parking lot.

The male officer spotted me. "Come out, Roxanne," he said quietly. I passed him his cap and he smiled. "You're a cheeky bugger, aren't you."

"Please don't take me back to Poiriua," I begged him.

"Okay, we'll see what we can do," he told me.

I was taken to Wellington police station once more. As soon as I got inside I heard someone say: "G'day, Roxanne." This time the police were exceptionally nice to me. Instead of restraining me they tried this different approach—and it worked. I was taken into a room, given some pens and paper, a hamburger, and an injection. The police contacted Poiriua Hospital, where they decided they didn't really want me back, then told me they were transferring me to Arohata Women's Prison. I was charged with escaping legal custody, stealing (the prescription pad) and usmg a document (writing out my prescriptions).

Arohata prison was a real shock: like Poiriua, it seemed medieval. I was forced to have a bath and then taken to a steel cell on the lower ground floor. There were bloodstains on the walls. I was told I would be in this cage for a few days.

I felt terrified. I couldn't see anything outside the cell. The only sound was the occasional rattle of the keys the screws carried as they walked past. There was no intercom system: if I had a panic attack I couldn't ask for help. I was so afraid, alone with my heartbeat. For the first twelve hours or so I still had Valium in my system, so I was okay. But then my brain began to spin out. As I lay on my bed I looked up and saw a barred grill above me. I twisted my blanket into a rope and tried to tie it around the bars, but I couldn't reach, I was too short. On the third day, one of the screws came to take me outside the cell for exercise. It was a joke. I was led away to empty my chamber-pot, then put back inside for another week.

When you suffer from a panic disorder, being alone in a locked room is a living nightmare. In 1989 my treatment at Arohata Prison seemed to me like abuse. After I'd been there eight days, I was told my father was on the telephone from Australia. James had tracked me down again. He told me he was fighting to help me and that I shouldn't give up. Just hearing his voice gave me a little hope.

Early next morning I was told I had to appear in court in Wellington. The screws gave me my clothes and some tea and toast. I knew I couldn't survive my court appearance without numbing my mind, so I smashed my cup and slashed my arm.

"We don't take any nonsense," one of the screws told me. She dragged me to the nurse, who bandaged me up and gave me some Valium.

I was taken by police car to the Wellington court cells. There a girl called Kylie told me I was entitled to bail and should get myself a lawyer. When Kylie's lawyer arrived I introduced myself to her. Celeste was sympathetic and seemed to me like a mother figure. When she heard how I'd been treated at Arohata, she said she wouldn't allow me to go back there, and would try to organise bail for me. Although I didn't have a home, Celeste told the magistrate I needed access to proper medical and psychological care. She made a few phone calls to the Lower Hutt Hospital, and bail was approved.

Celeste took me to her home. She lived as a single mother with her daughter Nikki, who was ten, and her teenage son, Matthew. She tried to treat me like one of her own children. While I was at Celeste's place I broke into a local doctor's surgery. My withdrawal symptoms from Valium had become massive. Yes, I felt guilty, but as a drug addict my behaviour was irrational. Celeste knew I was taking drugs. She told me to stop, otherwise she would take me back to the hospital. When she said that I cracked up. "You're just like everyone else in my life!" I screamed at her. "You don't want me!" I grabbed a razor and ran off.

I tried to swallow my feelings, but the anger inside me was immense. I walked around the suburbs for a while and eventually went into a school playground to rest. I knew that Celeste wouldn't want me back. I was too dangerous, too out of control.

I sat on a bench and slashed my arms with the razor. Then I lay down and closed my eyes. It was very early in the morning; in a few hours, I thought, the playground would be full of children laughing and playing. And here was I, with my life totally screwed up. Then I decided to call Celeste and see if she would take me back.

Celeste told me to come home. She had sent Matthew out to look for me, but she hadn't called the police. Slowly I walked back to her house and met Matthew on the way. He was sympathetic and told me his mum really did care about me, but she didn't know how to cope with me. When we reached the house, I saw flashing blue lights. The cops were there. I wanted to run but I was so tired. The police asked me whether I intended to do anything stupid to myself. As they waited for me to answer, I felt blood trickling from my arm, and pulled down my sleeve. Luckily they never noticed, and I told them I wouldn't hurt myself. Celeste had asked the police to give me a firm talking-to.

Celeste told me to go to bed and because I was so stoned she helped me to undress. Of course she noticed my arm. "Roxanne, what have you done to yourself!" I tried to tell her, but I was too confused. That night I slept like a log. Maybe because I felt I was in a real family house. Next morning Celeste told me she had to go away for a time, but would take me to a safe home to stay. I was grateful to her, I knew she had tried her best to cope with me, but what I needed was a team of people to help me.

We drove from the house and Celeste dropped her daughter off at a gym, then took me to a suburb called Island Bay. I had no idea where I was going, but she assured me I would be in good hands. As we drove over a high bridge, I looked far out over the ocean—it was the most magnificent view. We pulled into a courtyard and there before me I saw the Star of the Sea Convent. "No way!" I shouted. "There's no way I'm going to live with a bunch of nuns!" I felt as though I was back in the Convent of the Nativity in Sittingbourne, England, where I had been sent as a boarder so long ago.

I was taken inside and introduced to Sister Mary. I felt shocked to be there, but Celeste told me I had no choice: it was either the convent or else the police station. She gave the nuns my Valium and they showed me to my room. The view from the window was spectacular. I told Celeste I would try to be good, but I knew the moment the nuns' backs were turned I would be hightailing it out of here.

In the psychiatric ward at Lower Hutt Hospital I'd met a young guy called Howard. He had been discharged and had gone back to his parents in Wellington. He was a bit slow, but a very genuine person. He had given me his phone number. Now I snuck into one of the convent offices and called him. I begged him to come over, and told him to bring a bottle of Scotch with him. He duly arrived and I sneaked the Scotch up to my room. Sister Mary told me Howard could stay for dinner, but then he had to leave. After dinner I told him to wait in the garden. Back in my room, I opened the window and he climbed up the drainpipe. I told him that because Celeste had taken away all my pills I was going out to find some. Before we headed off together we polished off the bottle of Scotch.

Howard seemed to know his way around and led me to a doctor's surgery close by. I told him to keep an eye out while I broke in. I smashed a window and climbed through it. Inside I found hundreds of pills, including Valium, Serapax and Normison. Within seconds, an alarm went off. We ran back to the convent and climbed up to my room. The nuns must have been heavy sleepers, because we made a terrible noise. We spent the rest of the night getting stoned.

Next morning, Sister Mary called me for breakfast. I knew that if the nuns found Howard in my room, I would be sent straight back to gaol. I managed to stuff him into the wardrobe and told him to stay there until I'd had breakfast. Then he was to sneak around to the front door and pretend he had just arrived to see me.

As I walked into the breakfast room I was greeted quietly. I waited for someone to mention Howard, but it didn't happen. *My God*, I thought, *I've actually got away with it.*

I asked the nuns if I could leave the table. Sister Mary told me she wanted me to help with the dishes. I told her I just needed to go to my room to fetch something. It was the perfect time to tell Howard to sneak out. Then I returned to the kitchen to help clean up. My legs still felt wobbly because of all the drugs I'd taken. Presently Sister Mary came in and told me I had a visitor. I looked at her in surprise and went out to say hello to Howard.

The convent was a lovely double-storeyed building dating back to the early 1960s. It was surrounded by the beautiful blue sea. From my room I looked out on a small island with a volcano. White clouds hovering above it seemed to give it a magic element—or maybe that was just the drugs in my system. Staying in the convent had its moments. One night I asked Sister Mary if I could go out, and she said no. I told her she couldn't stop me. With a heap of pills in my bag I slammed the door and walked out. I found a bar in the city—I was the only girl there, surrounded by about twenty members of a local gang called Black Power. A Maori guy bought me a few drinks. I tried to call Howard, but his parents wouldn't let me speak to him. I sat in the pub until it closed, then stumbled outside. A few of the gang had got involved in a brawl and soon forgot about me.

...."Wake up, love," someone said. I woke to find two policemen standing over me, trying to rouse me. *Shit*, I thought. They asked my name and address. I said I was Tala Roberts, from Mangarie, and they seemed to buy it. They told me if I was still around the area next time they came past they would arrest me.

Struggling to my feet was an achievement. I had no idea

where to go. I stuck my thumb out, hoping someone would pick me up. Sure enough they did.

"Roxanne!" someone called. I turned around to see a police car, and tried to run, but they grabbed me. "You've been reported missing and we're taking you back to the convent," one of the cops told me. Apparently when Sister Mary phoned the police she said I was a suicidal risk. I was driven back to the convent to find Sister Mary waiting up like any concerned mother. In a strange way, I was beginning to like her.

Next day Sister Mary took me shopping. I asked her what nuns did for fun, and she told me they prayed. I told her to give me a break. She bought some material so that I could learn to sew. When we got back to the convent I sat at the sewing machine learning how to make a dress, which kept me nicely occupied for a couple of days.

During the second week at the convent, Celeste came to visit me. She told me I was to appear at Wellington Central Court next day on my three charges. I was scared. I feared I might be locked up in Arohata Prison again. That night I slashed my wrist, the fear was too strong. Sister Mary rushed me to hospital and waited with me while I had my wrist stitched. For some crazy reason whenever I hurt myself I felt better. Sister Mary was very worried about my behaviour. I don't think the convent had ever experienced anyone as wild as I was.

Celeste came again next day and assured me I wouldn't go back to gaol. As we left the convent for the court hearing I hung on to her. I still felt so scared. We sat together in the court and I asked Celeste if I could stay with her again. She told me she thought it would be possible, so long as I behaved. That meant obeying three major rules: no self mutilation, no drug-taking and no running away.

My case was heard and the magistrate decided to drop all the charges against me, providing I volunteered to leave the country and stayed in Celeste's custody until I left New

Zealand. I wasn't exactly deported, just kindly told to piss off. While I was at the Central Court I was informed that Sister Mary was in tears at Wellington police station. The Australian Consulate had refused me re-entry to Australia without a police clearance document.

By the following morning everything was sorted out and my visa was granted. I don't think the consulate had ever had to deal with a crying nun before. As Celeste, Sister Mary and the police escorted me to the airport I shed a few tears as well. I wondered why Sister Mary had bothered to come. I thought it was to make sure I had left the country, but as we said goodbye she said that she cared about me, and I think she really did. Sitting in the plane waiting for take-off, tears streamed down my face. I felt as though I wanted to stay. For some strange reason I had come to love New Zealand.

tasmania

❧

A late afternoon thunder storm greeted me as I arrived back in Sydney. As the plane touched down I wondered if the police would be there to meet me. Even though I had kept in contact with James, he hadn't mentioned the court situation. If a hearing had been scheduled and I'd failed to appear, I would be arrested immediately for skipping bail. But they were not there. I took a cab to James's house, anticipating that I would be thrown out when I arrived. It didn't happen. Except for a real good talking-to, James told me everything would be all right. He really cared about me. What other man would have put up with me? I thought he qualified for a sainthood. I wasn't the only street kid he had looked after, he had opened his heart and his home to others in need.

There were now only two days to go before I had to return to Minda; my allotted time in James's care, as stipulated by Rod Blackmore, the magistrate at Bidura Court, was almost up. In spite of the fact that James was still there for me, I remained aware of a powerful urge to be on the run again. I tried to ignore it. As we had lunch, James explained that the Department of Community Services was still threatening to go out on strike if in fact I was returned to Minda. In view of this and because I was on bail for armed robbery, it was likely I would have to go back to Mulawa Women's Prison.

That night I made a decision to call the television program

A Current Affair and tell my story. I really did want to get better but I needed so much help. Going on television would help me to get my message across. The following morning I called Channel Nine and spoke to Peter Wilkinson. He promptly agreed to do an interview with me as the most uncontrollable girl in New South Wales—according to the Department of Community Services.

I told James about this, and he warned me there could be unexpected consequences, but I was determined to be heard. He said he thought he should be there while I was interviewed. Peter Wilkinson carried out the interview at the Channel Nine studios. The program was to go to air the next evening. I'd taken half-a-dozen Valium to help me get through the ordeal. During the interview my identity was concealed, but I knew it was bound to come out later.

For a long time I had wanted to tell James the truth about myself—about my life in Western Australia and my true age. I had never had the guts to do it, but now I felt the time had come.

"James, please sit down," I said after we arrived home again. "I have something to tell you." He looked at me strangely as he perched on a stool at the kitchen counter. I told him I would quite understand if he didn't want anything more to do with me after he heard what I had to say. He smiled and asked me whether I'd once been male and changed sex—or, more seriously, whether I had AIDS. I shook my head.

"Roxanne, whatever it is we'll cope with it," he said. "I'm not going to abandon you."

'James," I told him, "My name's not Roxanne and I'm not seventeen. My name is Elizabeth, I'm wanted by the Western Australian police from way back, and I'm twenty-one." There, I'd said it.

James nearly fell off his stool. I think it was the shock of realising that I had fooled so many people—police, journalists, the Welfare Department. But he also realised that what I had told him did not change the person I was. (Though sometimes I wasn't sure myself who I was.) I went on to tell James my full life story, about my childhood abuse, growing up in Nyandi, and everything else I'd kept bottled up inside me for so long. I felt enormously relieved. I was sick of all the lies.

Suddenly James realised that *A Current Affair* would be shown in Western Australia, and I would be recognised by the authorities there. I told him it didn't matter, but he insisted that the program should be stopped for my own protection. He called Channel Nine immediately, and was told in no uncertain terms that the program would be shown whether he liked it or not. Then he called Lisa, my Welfare worker, and told her. She suggested obtaining a court injunction, since to all intents and purposes I was still a minor. We tried our best to stop the program going to air, but Channel Nine would not withdraw it.

Next morning, I was taken back to Minda. I hoped and prayed that by some miracle the Minda staff would not see the television program, but I knew there wasn't much hope of that.

That night the program was shown and the Minda staff saw my interview. I realised they must have received heaps of phone calls as a result: after the program ended the telephone didn't stop ringing, and the attitude of the staff towards me seemed strange. Afterwards, I heard that the Department of Community Welfare in Perth had been in contact with Channel Nine and with Minda. The Minda staff must have been stunned to learn the truth about my identity. The funniest thing of all was that I had worn my medic alert bracelet from the day I left Western Australia. It carried my identification number and a telephone number: at any stage the authorities could have dialled that number and found out who I really was. No one had ever bothered.

Next morning I was given a couple of pills and ordered to get dressed. I asked what was happening and was told to shut up. I soon found out. I was taken to Bidura Children's Court in Glebe for the last time, where the magistrate ordered that I should reside with James and that all my pending charges be dismissed.

Even though I was an adult, I was still very much a child. James decided he was going to set down some very strict rules. It was so good to be relieved of the Welfare department. Technically I was free, but emotionally I was chained to James—and to John. Every now and then he would call me and tell me how much I needed him. James encouraged me to stay at school and I did feel this gave me a chance I had missed before. The headmaster at Barrenjoey High School was a wonderful man, and the teachers gave me a lot of support. Three months after I returned to school, I was contacted by *60 Minutes*, who wanted to film a fifteen minute segment about my life. I wasn't so keen, but they offered me $3000. It took three weeks to film-and a lot of Valium. After it went to air I was suddenly seen at school as a celebrity.

The *60 Minutes* story covered many aspects of my life, including the time when I had stowed away on a visiting US warship in Perth. But even though I became semi-famous in the Palm Beach area, I felt my life was still in tatters. I did not want always to be known as the notorious "Roxanne". As a result of all this I felt I had to get away.

I had also gone back to the Narrabeen Youth Theatre, where I tried to express my emotions, but it still didn't work very well. When I was at Narrabeen one day, a young guy called Joey who I had often talked to approached me. He told me he was having problems at home. His parents wanted him to be more confident and hoped that attending the Youth Theatre would help. He told me he hated the Theatre. I liked Joey a lot, he was like the brother I'd never had. Although he was only seventeen, he seemed quite mature. When I talked to him about my life, he reckoned I was lucky to have James. I agreed, but I told him that I still felt an overpowering urge to run. Then I asked him if he, too, wanted to take off for a while. Rather surprisingly, he said yes. Without any delay we grabbed our gear and headed off to Sydney Airport. I asked him where he wanted to go. He said he didn't really care so long as we were together.

We found we had enough money for two one-way tickets to Tasmania. We boarded the plane and sat holding hands. I loved flying, but Joey was nervous, so I offered him a Valium and swallowed five myself. We didn't know what we'd do when we arrived, but we didn't care. Three hours later we touched down in Launceston. By this time James would probably have realised I was missing. I wondered what he was thinking. It was bloody freezing in Launceston and joey and I found a small cafe where we sipped hot coffee and wondered where we were going to sleep. I told him we should have brought overcoats. We hadn't realised how cold Tasmania was.

We found it a bit depressing in Launceston. The buildings all seemed old and drab.

"I'm going to break into some place and find a couple of blankets and a feed," I said. Joey agreed to keep watch while I selected a building to enter. I was as scared as hell. My legs were shaking and my heart was beating fast. Breaking into places was my least favourite crime. I would have felt better doing an armed hold-up. I searched around the place and found a window, but it was locked. Joey watched as I smashed the glass, then we both lay low for five minutes just in case one of the neighbours had called the police. Nothing happened, so I climbed in. Joey had a pocket torch which helped me see my way around. In one room there were two desks and a huge filing cabinet. There didn't seem to be any food, just a small tea urn and a fridge with a carton of milk. I opened one of the cabinets and looked through a few files. I nearly passed out.

"Joey," I said softly, "you'll never guess what this place is we've broken into. The Department of Probation and Parole!"

We decided to trash the place, we burnt most of the files then fled.

We knew we had to get out of Launceston, so we hit the road and stuck out our thumbs. It didn't take long before a guy who looked like a hippie picked us up. He told us we could crash at his place for the night. As we pulled into the place where he lived I remarked to Joey that it wasn't exactly the Hilton. Reggie lived in a two-bedroom hovel with dirty floors and cockroaches running everywhere. He threw us a mouldy blanket, then told us that he had a cupboard full of illegal firearms. Reggie definitely seemed ten cents short of a dollar. When he said this, Joey looked at me and I knew exactly what he was thinking. Reggie hit the sack fairly early, so I told Joey to get ready. We opened the door, took one of his guns, then quickly slipped out of there.

I was pleased we had a gun. I felt safer. Joey told me he thought he should hold it because I was too stoned, and he was right. I suddenly recalled that time in Wollongong by the railway tracks. I'd almost blown my foot off.

"Okay, you hold the gun," I agreed.

We walked for ages, for about twenty kilometres, then spotted a farmhouse some distance from the road. It looked like the ideal place to rob. Quietly I lifted the gate latch and we sneaked around to the barnyard. The night was pitch-black. It was a pretty old farmhouse, in the barn the owner had all his tools and farm equipment hanging from huge beams. As the wind blew it set up a spine-tingling howl. Joey tapped me on the shoulder and pointed to two oilskin jackets. We grabbed them and decided it was time to get out of the place. We could have slept in the barn, but we thought that maybe it was haunted.

We went on walking along the Bass Highway until we came to a small town called Oatlands, where we finally lay down to sleep in a grassy area. Neither of us got much sleep, however. Around six in the morning we got up and found a small cafe. Joey ordered a hamburger with the lot. I had a coffee and four Valium. It wasn't long before once again I was drugged to the eyeballs.

Joey suggested our best plan was to return to Launceston and find a hostel, so we set off and walked all the way back again. I told him to hide the gun just in case were were stopped by the police. As we walked around Launceston wearing our oilskin jackets and Akubra hats, we were stopped by a photographer to asked if he could take photos of us for the local paper. It didn't seem a good idea to have our photos plastered all over the paper, so we said no...only to see him taking our picture from across the road.

After our two seconds of fame we searched for accommodation. The youth hostel was booked out, so we sat in a carpark and prayed for a miracle. I thought about calling James to let him know I was in Tasmania and okay, but I thought he might tell me to get lost. I knew perfectly well that I had messed up all the opportunities he had given me. As he'd told me, I would never get better unless I went to a rehabilitation hospital and stopped using drugs.

I turned to Joey. "Listen, if you want to go home, I'll understand." I knew his parents would be worried and I didn't want him to end up in trouble. But he agreed to stick with me. We didn't want to be seen walking around with the shotgun, so we hid it beside some garbage bins, then left the carpark and walked back into the town. I was very stoned; it only took one look to see how drugged I was. Before we reached the next corner we were pulled over by two police officers. They asked us where we were from. I told them we were backpackers from the mainland. The cop asked me what drug I was on, and asked for identification. Joey had been reported missing by his parents, and after the cops had checked on their two-way radio he was taken into custody. He told the police he'd met me in Victoria, and because I wasn't wanted there they had to let me go.

My clothes and personal effects were in the rucksack Joey was carrying, and before he handed it over to me the police searched through it. I whispered to Joey to say nothing about the break-and-enter or the gun. He nodded and then the cops took him away.

I sat across the road from the youth hostel wondering what to do next. I swallowed some more pills and took out my razor. Feeling sorry for myself, I gently slashed my wrist until little streams of blood ran out. I felt confused. Why did I resort to such primitive behaviour? I felt that I didn't belong anywhere. The only stability I'd ever known was behind locked doors.

I knew that my fingerprints were all over the shotgun and I didn't want it to fall into the wrong hands. I'd noticed a poster advertising a gun amnesty—no questions asked if you sur-rendered any illegal weapons to the police, so I thought the best thing would be to drop the gun off at the local cop shop. I managed to retrieve it from the carpark and tried to walk as inconspicuously as possible, hiding it under my oilskin coat. When I reached the police station I marched right in with the gun in my hand.

When the officer behind the counter saw me he dived out of sight. "Put it down!" he yelled. The poor man was terrified.

"Okay, okay," I said. "I'm here to hand over this gun." There was another amnesty poster in the station and I drew his attention to it as I laid the shotgun on the counter.

He took a deep breath. "You scared me, love. We get all kinds in here."

I turned and ran out. Within a few minutes I was sur-rounded by cops. They told me I was under arrest and took me back to the police station, where I was questioned at length. "We arrested your boyfriend, Joey, this morning," they said, "and he informed us you were involved in a burglary with him." *Fuck*, I thought. I couldn't believe Joey had squealed.

"Yeah, I did—so what?" I said.

By way of reply I was strip-searched and thrown into a cold steel cell. "I want my medication!" I screamed. "If you don't give it to me I'll hang myself!" They didn't give me the pills, instead they told me if I didn't quieten down I would be stripped and left to freeze all night without a blanket. The station food was disgusting. I threw it at the wall. The police had taken everything away from me, so I had no razor to slash myself. After a cold night I was taken before a Justice of the Peace, who ordered that I be taken to Risdon Prison, in Hobart. I was thrown in a police wagon and escorted to gaol.

On arrival at Risdon I was strip-searched as usual, taken to a cell and given a nightie. One of the prison officers questioned me about all the scars on my arms. I burst out crying and told her I wanted to die. I hated being caged like an animal, but at the same time I feared the outside world. She grabbed me and pushed me into the cell. I screamed all night to be let out. I couldn't breathe. Everything was spinning out of control. I was hysterical. Finally, in the early hours of the morning, the Governor, Mrs Biles, came to my cell and I was taken off to an isolation shed in the garden area of the prison, where I was forcibly held down and given an injection. Whatever it was, it knocked me out for two days.

Finally I woke in a sweat. I had no idea what day it was. The Governor was a tough Scottish woman in her fifties. She hadn't bothered to read my medic alert bracelet, which showed I was allergic to certain medications. I heard the clanking of keys and an officer brought me a tray with bread and tea. Then in walked the Governor again, and gave me another injection. My mouth became dry and within minutes I felt I was floating out of my body. It was really frightening. I tried to call for help but the words wouldn't come.

Finally, I was locked in a cell in the mainstream area of the prison, and within a few days I was taken to appear at the Launceston Court House. Lying in a cell there, I thought about my mother. I wondered whether she knew I was still alive. What would she think if she knew I was sitting in a dark cell at the other end of Australia? In the court room the charges against me were read out, and the magistrate also read out a number of reports, including one from James recommending that I be detained so that I could detox from drugs. I was asked how I wished to plead, guilty or not guilty. I replied I didn't care, I was going to be locked up anyway. Then the magistrate passed sentence and ordered me to serve one month. I spent the night in the cells and was given a meal Her Majesty would have been proud of—cold sausage, a piece of bread, and a cup of weak coffee.

Next day I was returned to Risdon, where the Governor called me into her office. She told me I was to sleep in my own cell and mix with the other prisoners, but if I played up I would be taken to the isolation hole. That first day back I spent alone in the sewing room, though why they called it that I don't know. There were no sewing-machines and we weren't allowed scissors. Then one of the prison officers told me I was to be transferred to the Royal Tasmanian Hospital, because the Risdon staff considered me a suicide risk, and thought my behaviour was more like that of a fifteen-year old than an adult criminal. I didn't really mind going to yet another psych hospital, but I wasn't exactly looking forward to it, either.

The Royal Tasmanian Hospital looked like a relic left over from convict days. I was taken to the main locked ward and put in an isolation cell until the next day, when I was allowed to enter the main ward area. It was very disturbing: there were at least twenty patients who just sat staring into space, a man who thought he was an aeroplane and walked around going *vroom, vroom*, and a young girl who looked as though she had anorexia nervosa. She spent all day sitting on the floor rocking backwards and forwards.

I found a plastic chair and joined the other patients. There were no magazines to read, only a television high up on the wall, with a metal grill over the screen so that it couldn't be broken. The nurses decided what we could watch. This was the security ward, designed to keep the most severely affected patients in protective custody. A door opened out into a big garden, but there were no trees, just dried-up lawn and a high brick wall.

The security ward was frightening. Every morning I was woken by the nurses, and forced to take a bath—if I refused, they held me down and washed me. I saw one nurse deliberately hold the anorexic girl's head under water after she splashed them. I made friends with one of the male patients, Gavin. He told me he was in the hospital because he suffered from schizophrenia. He told me the hospital was really bad, that they abused the patients all the time.

After the first week I settled into a routine of the morning bath, mealtimes, medication and sleep. I got to know a few of the staff who didn't seem so bad. One male nurse, Harley, was very kind to the patients. I was seen by a psychiatrist and told her about my agoraphobia and my panic attacks. She didn't seem very interested, but told me she would put me on a drug called phnalzine because I was depressed. There was a twenty-minute exercise routine each day which no one wanted to do, but we had to, otherwise we didn't get our cigarettes. The nurses handed out smokes every hour to their favourite patients.

During my second week, Anthony, a new night nurse, came on duty. He used to look at me and smile. Usually every patient had to be locked in their room at night, but I had been given permission to sleep with my door left open, because I felt so claustrophobic. One night around seven o'clock, Anthony called me over and told me to follow him. He led me though a few doors, then outside through the laundry, and in again to the office area at the front of the building. There he grabbed me. I was terrified. He bit me, put his hands around my throat and raped me. Afterwards he told me I must not tell anyone. If I did he said he would see I went into isolation and remained drugged. I would never leave the hospital.

After the rape I went back to my cell and cried. I kept a diary, and I wrote down what had happened. I tried my hardest not to cut myself. A female nurse came in and asked me why I was crying. I couldn't bring myself to tell her, I just curled up in bed and tried to black it out.

Anthony raped me again a week later. He came into my room while I was asleep and I woke with his hand over my mouth. I tried to fight him off, but he was lying on top of me. There was no way out of this nightmare. I wanted to tell someone, but I felt no one would believe me. I did tell Gavin, the schizo-phrenic patient, and he said I should write a letter and get it to the outside world. This seemed a rational idea, but it wasn't possible because the staff read all the mail. I hated Anthony and lived in fear whenever he was on duty.

One Friday he came on duty, walked into my room and gave me a tablet which he said was a cough lolly—he knew I had a cold. Later on, he called me and said there was a phone call for me. I hoped it was James, so that I could try to tell him what was happening. Anthony then took me into an office, unlocking and relocking the doors as we passed through the corridors. I walked over to the desk and picked up the phone. "Hello ..." I said. There was no one on the other end. Anthony pushed me up against the wall, his hands around my throat. The tablet he'd given me earlier had made me feel drowsy. After he finished the whole scene felt like a fantastic nightmare. He said he would kill me if I told anyone, and I knew then I had to find a way to escape.

We returned to the main room, and I asked Anthony if I

could borrow the keys to get myself a drink. The staff always handed us the keys because it was too much trouble for them to get up and unlock the doors. I grabbed the keys and ran to my room. I put on my jeans, took a few other things, and managed to remember the way Anthony had taken me through the hospital the first time he raped me. I opened the laundry door, locking it behind me, and ran out as fast as I could. I ran along a dark road until I found a phone box and called the operator, who put me through to James.

"James, you have to help me. I'm in the Royal Tasmanian Hospital and I've been raped," I told him.

Suddenly I heard a knock on the glass door of the phone box and a torch shone on my face. "Come out of there," a policewoman ordered me. "We're going to take you back to the hospital."

"No, please don't do that," I begged. "Please lock me up in your cells. I'd rather go to gaol!"

Constable Kenny told me she would take me back to New Norfolk police station and try to sort something out. I sat in the back of the police car, crying and shaking. I was terrified. I didn't know who to trust.

When we got to the station Constable Kenny sat with me in an interview room. She knew I was very upset. She asked the male constable present to leave the room, then asked me if I had something I wanted to tell her. She told me her name was Nicole. I said I couldn't go back to the hospital. "One of the nurses is raping me," I said. She asked me what had happened and how long it had been going on. I tried to tell her, but I was very distressed. She told me that what I was saying was a very serious matter, and warned me I could be in a lot of trouble if I was not telling the truth.

"I'm not lying, please help me. I'd rather be in the cells than go back there."

Finally Nicole told me she believed me, and a short time

later Sergeant Kemp, a detective, came in. I was asked to tell him everything. I told him how Anthony had repeatedly raped me. Sergeant Kemp was a caring man—apart from Detective Civich in Perth, he was the nicest policeman I'd ever encountered. He told me everything would be okay and he would do his best to help me. As I sat in the interview room I was told that the police had arrested Anthony for questioning and that he was in the next room.

Then I was driven to the Royal Hobart Hospital to be medically examined, which I found disgusting. They asked me lots of personal questions about my sex life. I felt utterly humiliated and couldn't stop crying. Being raped was the most traumatic experience of my life. Finally I received some good news. Anthony had admitted to having sexual intercourse with me. The police charged him, but there was nothing they could do to prevent me being taken back to the Royal Tasmanian Hospital, since I was under a court order.

Early next morning I was driven back and made to sleep in the alcoholic men's ward, with a nurse watching me all night. Next day I was escorted back to the security ward where I had been raped. Two male nurses took me to an isolation room and told me to hand over my clothes. I told them I wasn't getting undressed, so they forcibly stripped me and threw me a nightie. I couldn't believe the way they were treating me. I received no counselling and no apology. I was left alone in a cold cell for three days because I had told the police that Anthony had raped me.

Finally a miracle occurred. Nicole Kenny and Sergeant Kemp came to see me. They said they were sorry they hadn't been able to get me out of the hospital and asked me how I was being treated. I told them what was happening. After they left the hospital Superintendant told me I was being transferred to an open ward.

Ward 12 was another shock to the system; as I walked in,

a woman lifted up her dress at me—she wasn't wearing any underwear. I was told I would have a nurse with me for twenty-four hours every day. It seemed a bit late to give me a guard. The first two days I was placed in a room by myself, with the guard outside. The staff resented the way I had disrupted their crazy hospital. I sat in my room with a colouring book and wrote a few poems. Then I was told that Nicole had arrived to see me again. This time after her visit I was taken out of isolation and placed with the other patients. In fact Ward 12 was a lot better than the previous security ward. Patients were treated much better and there was even a psychologist on duty.

My agoraphobia and panic attacks became worse after I'd been raped. I didn't want to go out for walks, but the nurses forced me to take the exercise. I was told that if I didn't go I would be put in isolation.

One day two nurses took me with a group of other patients into New Norfolk for some shopping. I decided to buy a few clothes for a patient called Bryan. As we were standing in the menswear store waiting for change, a nurse tugged at my sleeve and told me to hurry. "Stop forcing me to do what you want!" I screamed. "You're all a bunch of bullies!" I felt so pressured that I grabbed my change and made a run for it.

I kept running until I saw a park, and as I ran across the road I heard someone call my name. I looked back and saw Nicole with a male constable. "Stop, Roxanne, it's me, Nicole!" she yelled, but I ran on into the park, where I sat wondering what I should do now. Tasmania was the worst place I'd ever been to. If it wasn't for Nicole and Sergeant Kemp I would probably have killed myself after the rape. I didn't feel safe. I wanted to get my clothes and other things from the hospital and fly home to Sydney, but it seemed as though the hospital just wouldn't let me go.

Nicole and the other constable walked over to me and said that everything would be okay. I cried as I told Nicole how much I hurt inside, and how I felt I couldn't trust anyone. Being raped had left me feeling betrayed and violated, in the same degrading way that Allen had made me feel all those years ago when I was a child. After listening to me, Nicole drove me back to the hospital. There was no good reason why I should stay there. I told her I was going to get my property and discharge myself. I had originally been sentenced to one month, but had now served four.

After a battle with the nurses I was given my belongings. I caught a taxi to the airport. Sitting in the plane up above the clouds was the most wonderful feeling in the world. As I closed my eyes a feeling of freedom filled my body. I looked out of the window and watched as Tasmania turned into a tiny speck and finally disappeared from sight.

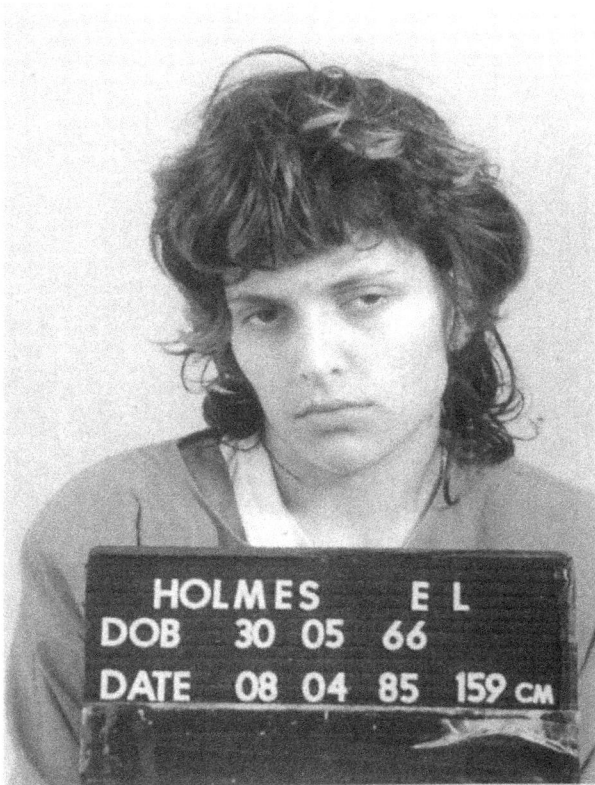

HOLMES   E L
DOB 30 05 66
DATE 08 04 85 159 cm

HOLMES E L
DOB 30 5 66

BAIL UNDERTAKING

Rozanne Lee

Act and

40/1900

NAME OF ACCUSED:

ADDRESS OF ACCUSED

Short title of Offence(s).

Assault with intent to robe

Gosford: On the run from the police, I contemplated my whole life beside the fence. After this photo was taken I slashed my wrists and took an overdose: I felt so alone, so sad, and prayed that someone would love me.

During the filming of 60 Minutes, Geoff McMullen wouldn't stop asking me all those hardhitting questions ... I decided he needed a little silencing. In the midst of my laughter I realised the TV camera was still rolling.

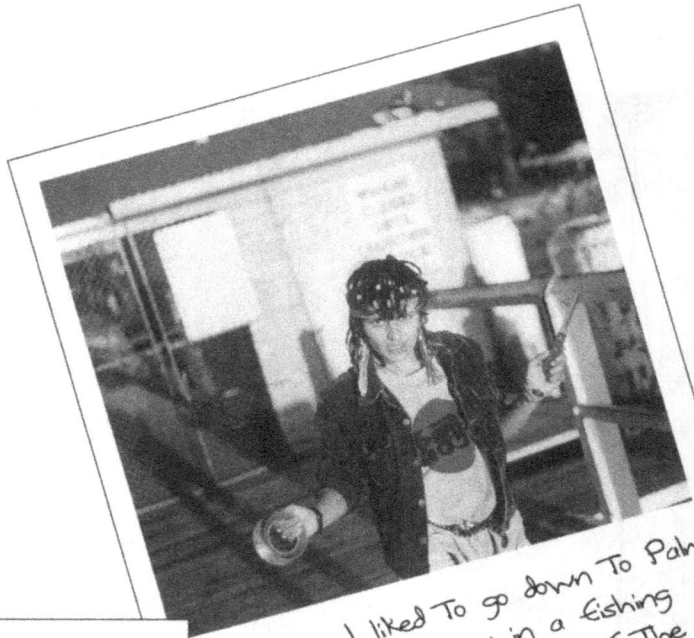

SomeTimes I liked To go down To Palm Beach wharf, Throw in a fishing line and Try To make sense of The mad world I was Trapped in.

The Lion Safari Park, Sydney: I wanted To recapTure my childhood. Even Though I was The oldesT rider on The carousel, I Think I had The mosT fun.

James, Jesse and I on our way To The Basin near Palm Beach.

Posing for Heidi Herbert with Arizona, at Whale Beach I wanted this photo to capture my daughter's beauty and innocence.

Palm Beach, Sydney: Arizona's first birthday was fantastic I got to experience the simple joy of being a mum, I prepared all the food myself, but went a bit overboard on the Smarties.

1996:
Contemplating my
future ...
wondering where
my life will take
me from here. I
still have dreams
of one day opening
a home for unloved
and abused children.

home

∽

I felt very apprehensive about returning to James after all the trouble I had put him through. At Sydney Airport I caught a taxi back to Palm Beach and James's place and knocked at the door.

"Rox!" he cried, "you're back!" He wrapped his arms around me and gave me a hug. It was wonderful to know he truly cared about me. He had painted my bedroom a beautiful shade of ocean blue—he said he had known I would soon be home. I decided I was going to stay for a while. Travelling and running wild were just too stressful. I felt as though I had been running all my life.

Every morning, James and I talked. I came to realise that I did have a serious drug dependency and a bad problem with self-mutilation. James told me I must go to a drug rehabilitation centre, otherwise I would be a drug addict forever. He said he would always love and support me, but I must stop hurting myself and find more appropriate ways to deal with my emotions. We made a deal that whenever I felt extreme fear, panic or anger, instead of cutting my arms I would approach him and we would talk about it. He said that if I felt I was about to have a panic attack, I shouldn't just take drugs, I should ask for help. It sounds all too easy in theory, but the reality was another matter. I had never found it easy to talk about my feelings. My mother had instilled in me that it was wrong to talk about how you felt or to show emotion. I had always been too scared to know happiness. I was really only comfortable with absolute fear and apprehension.

It was now almost a month since I left Tasmania, and I was beginning to feel more secure. The rape had been a horrific event and I had constant flashbacks and nightmares. Sometimes, too terrified to go to sleep, I would deliberately lie awake in a cold sweat. During these nights I tried hard to rationalise my thoughts. I felt as though I was to blame for what had happened. I felt worthless and dirty. Once again I began to take showers wearing my clothes. I hated my body and the way I looked.

I tried very hard to forget about Tasmania, but I couldn't. My thoughts seemed to be trapped in a web, spinning out of control. I came to the conclusion that all I could do was to live one day at a time and get through it as best I could.

One day I received a call from my solicitor, Anne Marie. I was to appear in court at Manly next day in relation to the armed hold-up at the chemist's shop in Narrabeen. That evening I sat in my room and played my favourite Prince album. I swallowed a few pills and once more contemplated ending my torturous existence. I wrote a suicide note. It seemed as thought there was no other answer.

James called me for dinner but I told him I wasn't hungry. I went into the bathroom, found a razor, then returned to my bedroom and began to slash my arms. The blood didn't really scare me and my mind was numb to the pain. The main sensation was one of all my tension and confusion disappearing, flowing out of me in a rush.

Fifteen minutes later the guilt trip arrived. I always felt guilty afterwards. I knew I was letting James down. I ran into the bathroom to wash off the blood—some of the cuts were deep but others were merely scratches. I found a bandage and tried to hide the mass of cuts by putting on a long sleeved shirt.

"Come on, Rox," said Jesse, my young adopted brother. "Come and have dinner. We've got chips tonight." Jesse was such a great kid. He was so unselfish—he'd allowed me into his home and shared his dad with me. Most of the time I seemed to demand all the attention, and poor Jesse would be left in the background. Every night Jesse, James and I would eat together as a family. James had a rule that no television was to be watched during meal times, so we often sat just watching and listening to the waves crashing along Palm Beach. These times form my most treasured memories.

That evening, sharp-eyed James spotted blood dripping onto the floor. "Rox, what have you done?" he asked. He pulled up my sleeve, saw the injuries then gave me a big hug. "Oh Rox, you know you don't have to hurt yourself like this."

I fell against his chest and howled like a child. "I want to die. Please let me die." I felt so much pain inside that it seemed impossible to go on. I felt as though I would explode from carrying my sadness around with me for so long.

James knew that sometimes he couldn't help me—this was my pain, not his. As I lay on my bed he went into his office and I heard him make a telephone call. Then he came to my room. "I've called the Mona Vale police," he told me, "and they're coming to take you to the station. It's simply for your own protection until the court hearing is over. I'm very worried about your behaviour."

Soon two police officers arrived to take me away. "Just let me get dressed," I told them.—"Okay, but leave your bedroom door slightly open," one of them said. I heard him ask James if there was a doorway outside my room, and James said there wasn't. Slowly I opened my bedroom window as I yelled out to the cops "I'm almost ready!" Then I jumped out into the bushes four metres below. One of the cops heard the noise. "Christ, she's jumped," he said. He jumped out of the window too and practically landed on top of me. "Come on, Roxanne, you're going to the station," he told me.

The police vehicle was waiting at the top of the driveway. It was a big F 100 van, and I was told to sit in front between the two officers. Even though they were treating me well, I was still scared. We left Palm Beach and as we were passing through Newport a call came over the radio to attend a property where a motorbike had been stolen. We pulled up outside the house and the officers told me to sit in the car like a good girl. As they walked across the road I saw that the keys were still in the ignition. *What do I do now?* I thought. The cops were looking back at me, so I pretended to yawn and stretching out both my arms, I locked the doors. Then I moved into the driving seat and started the motor.

"Fuckin' hell!" yelled one of the police officers.

They both ran over to the car.

"Roxanne, open the door!" they shouted. They pulled out their batons and threatened to break the window.

I had never driven such a big vehicle and was having trouble with the gears.

"Come on, Roxanne, this isn't fair. We'll lose our jobs," one of them said.

I felt sorry for them then and wanted to open the doors, but I was scared they would lock me in the back. I went on trying to get the car moving. Then the cops told me that if I didn't get out they'd call for back-up and a road block. I managed to get my mind to make the right decision, but before I opened the doors I swallowed a handful of Valium and Normison, so that if they decided to bash me I wouldn't feel the pain.

Both officers breathed heavy sighs of relief as I opened the doors. They didn't bash me, in fact they were really understanding. When we reached Mona Vale police station Constable Pare, a senior officer, gave me a lecture on the effects of using and abusing drugs. I was put in an interview room and they asked me if I'd like a cup of coffee. I still had a heap of Valium in my pocket and knew I would be searched, so I brought out a handful and swallowed them. A cop spotted me doing this and asked what I had taken. The police doctor was called—he said I would be all right and would sleep it off. I curled up in a corner of the room and slept heavily.

The following morning I was escorted to Manly police station and put into the cells until it was time for the court hearing. I felt trapped. "Let me out!" I screamed, "I'm going to kill myself, I can't breathe!" The police monitored me with a video camera and called for James to calm me down. A doctor gave me a sedative, and then I was called into court.

The magistrate, Michelle Copeland, told me she wanted to adjourn the case but would refuse bail because it was a serious offence. The police prosecutor told her I was a danger to myself and might well take my own life. It was a crazy situation: I had found a new home with James but I kept messing it all up. I seemed to want to deny myself the chance of happiness.

That night the police took me back to the cells. My lawyer put in an immediate appeal and requested I be sent to a detoxification centre in Sydney. The magistrate granted the request. She told me she could see no future for me but death or continuing imprisonment unless I changed.

I was driven to the rehabilitation centre and told to get into bed. A urine test was taken, and I was told I wasn't allowed to go anywhere. The staff gave me the twelve steps from Alcoholics Anonymous, and as I read through them I began to see how much damage I had created towards myself and others in my life. I never wanted to be a bad person, and I don't believe my mother did either. I loved her still. I think we were both victims of circumstance. I really wanted to change and be a good person all the way along, but there was just too much happening to me all the time. I knew it was self-created, but I couldn't undo the mess. The web that I had spun was suffocating me.

I stayed in the rehab centre; it was a really hard emotional and physical struggle, but I did manage to get through it. There were days of headaches and depression and my mind would scream out for Valium, but I prayed and kept praying.

After I had finished my two months there I returned to James's house. Although I had stopped taking my other drugs, I was still taking the anti-depressant drug which the hospital in Tasmania had given me. Slowly I began to wean myself off this as well. Every morning James would take me to the beach to swim. It was wonderful. I also began a program with a local doctor to help me with the panic attacks. It wasn't easy changing from a wild child into a normal (well, almost normal) person. There were still many difficulties, but slowly I began to open up. I no longer overdosed and created havoc, and I began to gain a little respect from the people around me. Sometimes I was asked to baby-sit their children, and I was overjoyed that people trusted me to that extent. Slowly the community began to accept me.

One night, as I fell into an easy sleep something very strange happened to me. Around midnight I felt my body rising up, then floating. I looked down and saw myself lying on the bed. I felt an incredible sensation of warmth and peace. As I rose up an intense light filled my being and I heard a man's voice telling me that I wasn't ready to go yet, it wasn't my time, I still had things to do. When I woke up inside my earthly body, I was filled with fear and later called a priest. He told me I was fortunate to have had such a spiritual experience. Yes, I am lucky. I have been given a second chance in life.

Around this time I had been seeing a guy called Hugh. Although our affair was fairly lighthearted, we had an intimate relationship, which was very important for me. Hugh was tall and stocky, and I felt safe with him. About three months after we had been seeing each other, I began to feel pains in my breasts.

We discussed the possibility of pregnancy, and Hugh came with me to a shopping centre where we bought a pregnancy test. I went off to the toilet, applied the test, then waited there for the result. "Oh my God!" I cried out, "it's positive!" I tried to work out when my last period had been—it was at least two months ago. Then I asked Hugh to take me to the medical centre for a proper examination. The doctor was very understanding. He examined me and told me that I was six to eight weeks pregnant. He told me the baby's heart was already beating.

Hugh and I arranged to meet next day and then I went home and told James that I was pregnant. He seemed to take the news more easily than I did. We discussed the options. Although I hated the thought of an abortion, I had to consider it. As I lay awake in bed that night, I wondered about all the drugs I had taken in my life. Would they affect the unborn child? I felt a wave of guilt sweep over me.

Next morning I had pains in the stomach, so I called up the doctor. He said I needed to be examined, and sent me to a local hospital for tests. He suspected I might have an ectopic pregnancy, when the embryo is lodged in the fallopian tubes instead of inside the uterus. This can be life threatening for the mother and fatal for the embryo.

As James took me into the hospital I was scared. I wondered whether my baby would survive. A young nurse told me to get changed, and I told her I wanted to go home, but she persuaded me to stay. Then a grey-haired doctor came into the cubicle and asked me about my pregnancy. I was given a blood test, and he told me he wanted me to have a laparoscopy. He said it was a relatively simple procedure. A cut would be made into my umbilicus and a tube with a telescopic lens inserted through my navel. He would then be able to see whether the embryo was ectopic or not. I was handed a consent form for the operation, to which I assented. He also asked me if I would like to have my pregnancy terminated, and I said "no". I told him I was there to save the pregnancy, not get rid of it. Then I was put into a white gown and wheeled into the theatre. I lay on the operating table and the anaesthetist picked up my hand and said he was going to give me a needle in it. He told me to count back from ten. "Ten—nine—eight ..." I counted, then everything went black.

I awoke in bed. As I opened my eyes the nurse told me I was in the recovery ward.

"How's my baby?" I asked.—"Just try to rest, love," was the response. "The doctor will be here to see you in the morning."

I wondered why she had not answered my question. I was given a sedative and fell back into sleep.

Early next morning the doctor came and I asked him how my baby was.

"Roxanne, you weren't pregnant," he told me.

"What!" I exclaimed. "Don't try to tell me that. Why do you think I was admitted?"

He told me to get dressed and go home, and insisted that I had never been pregnant.

Then I discovered that I was bleeding. "You've given me an abortion, haven't you?" I asked the doctor.

He told me I would never be able to prove it, and then he discharged me.

I couldn't reach James or Hugh by phone, so I caught a taxi to a friend's place. Tearfully I poured out the whole story to Camilla, who agreed that it seemed as though the doctor had terminated my pregnancy without my per mission, then thought he could get away with it by using the excuse that I was never pregnant in the first place. However, he didn't realise that I had been seen by two other doctors, both ofwhom had confirmed my pregnancy.

Eventually I reached James and told him what had happened. He called my local doctor, who said he already knew about the termination. He told James that the doctor at the local hospital had terminated my pregnancy because he thought I wasn't the kind of girl who should have a baby. Apparently he had seen me on the *60 Minutes* program and had decided to play God.

Over the next few weeks I fell into a depression and had severe panic attacks. James told me that although I had had my pregnancy unlawfully aborted, I had to try to get on with my life. I enrolled in Kuring-gai College but found it hard to study. This was one of the most depressing periods of my life. I was devastated that I had been denied the chance to give birth. The doctor had made a personal decision to judge me as an unfit mother, basing his judgement on a fifteen-minute television documentary. How dared he rob me of my baby!

I battled as best I could. Hugh and I split up because of the stress and he went to Queensland. It was ten weeks now since the pregnancy had been aborted. Yet it was curious—I still felt as though I *was* pregnant. I made an appointment to see the local doctor and he told me I was going through a phantom pregnancy. He said losing a baby was often a very traumatic experience. "But Jeffrey," I told him, "I really do feel as though I'm pregnant." He refused to believe me.

James advised me to get a second opinion. The next day at college I almost fainted in a lecture. Donna, a student friend, helped me into the doctor's surgery. Dr Franklin told me that I needed a full examination and she gave me a number of blood and urine tests. I didn't tell her about the termination—just to talk about it made me feel so depressed. She told me I could be anaemic and might need some iron tablets. After I'd seen her I returned to my lectures, trying to put everything out of my mind.

When I got home that afternoon I found James had left a note to say he was in the city and wouldn't be back until late. I went into my room, curled up on my bed and listened to Prince. The time dragged by. I took off my clothes and got into my pyjamas. My tummy definitely seemed larger. But I knew that whether my baby was ectopic or not, it could never have survived dilation and the curette.

A couple of days later I went back to see Dr Franklin at college. There was a strange expression on her face. "Roxanne, you do realise you're pregnant, don't you?" she asked.

"What!" I exclaimed. "That's impossible." I hadn't had sex for several weeks before the termination. "You must have made a mistake," I said. Then I poured out the whole story to her. She was even more surprised than me, and showed me the test results which read: *serum pregnancy test—positive.*

My God, I'm still pregnant, I thought. All along, deep inside myself, I had known it was true. When Dr Franklin examined me she estimated I was three and a half months pregnant, which meant that I would have conceived at least five weeks or more before I went into hospital. I asked her for a copy of the blood test results.

I told Donna what had happened. She was shocked. I was so angry that I felt I had to go to the hospital and tell the doctor what I thought of him, and Donna said she would come with me. We arrived there later that afternoon. I walked into Casualty and spoke to the first doctor I saw. "So, I wasn't bloody pregnant!" I exclaimed, and called them all murdering bastards.

He ordered my file and even though he knew I was telling the truth, he tried to cover it up by saying I had not been pregnant before. Donna and I left the hospital after some heated words, then I caught a taxi home.

"James, James, I'm still pregnant, nearly four months!" I called out as I ran through the door.

He looked at the blood test result and was amazed. We then telephoned the local doctor, and he was amazed as well. I was booked in for an ultrasound at the hospital, where a very nice obstetrician examined me. He said I was thirty-two weeks pregnant.

My pregnancy was quite an emotional roller-coaster. If other people found it confusing, they could only guess how I felt, going through all that. There was only one person who had believed in me all the way along and that was Camilla. She'd always said that a woman knows her own body best. She was right— everyone else thought I was mistaken in saying I still felt pregnant after I'd had an abortion.

The following week I had to appear at the Sydney District Court, on the charge of demanding money with menaces. The magistrate called my name and I stood up before him. I was scared, but prepared to take my punishment. The magistrate seemed to know who I was from the *60 Minutes* program. He said he was able to empathise with me, and gave some details of his own life, which had once been similar to mine. He told me that he wanted me to experience some good in life and to give my child a good start. He gave me a three-year good behaviour bond, which I did not break.

enter arizona

❧

On 22 August I woke feeling contractual pains and told James my baby was on its way. He drove me to the Royal Women's Hospital in Paddington. Ten hours later my beautiful daughter, Arizona, came into the world. Nothing, no single event in my extraordinary life, had prepared me for childbirth. James sat behind me during labour, and my little brother Jesse gazed at the miracle unfolding before his eyes.

"Push, Roxanne, push!" yelled one of the nurses.

"I can't!" I yelled. It hurt like hell. A doctor appeared and injected a warm substance into my arm. As the Pethidine took effect, my tiny precious baby was making her way into the world.

At that moment a fleeting thought filled my consciousness: "I have survived." After all my suicide attempts, overdoses, jumping off buildings, after the armed robberies I had carried out and the time I'd spent in prison, I was allowed to experience the wonder of giving birth. I knew God was watching over me and protecting me; I believed He had a plan for me.

My body was suddenly jolted back into reality by a huge wave-like contraction that finally and amazingly brought my baby into the world. There was no fanfare, no fireworks, just a single moment that celebrated life and bonded us together. As I held my tiny baby, I gave thanks to God. She was a true miracle.

"Congratulations, Roxanne, you have a daughter." Gazing into her eyes, the noise around me seemed insignificant. As the doctor cut her umbilical cord and we were separated, it all seemed an incredible experience of great love.

Jesse asked me what I was going to call my daughter. I already knew. I had chosen the name Arizona—an American Indian word representing water. It was important for me to give her a name filled with love. I remembered very well how deprived I had felt when I discovered that I had been named Elizabeth just because that was the Queen's name!

I spent six days in the hospital, learning how to start being a mother. The nurses were wonderful: they really cared about me and my baby. Like all new mothers, I couldn't wait to leave the hospital. The first two weeks at home weren't easy. I began to experience panic attacks once more and lack of sleep sent me crazy. Arizona woke every four hours just like clockwork. No sooner had I got her to sleep than she would wake again. I was still dependent on sedatives, and I seemed to feel the joy of motherhood draining from my soul. Momentarily I was aware of the same feelings of rejection my mother had felt for me. I loved my child, but I felt as though I had lost control. Later that night I sat in my little room in James's house, overlooking the beach, with a big shot of Valium in my system. I grabbed a razor and cut my wrist, and as the blood ran down my arm, anger flooded my body. I hated myself. I wanted to be a good mother, always in control, but now I was terrified I would end up just like my mother. The five Valium pills I'd swallowed had made me tired. I hadn't taken any pills in hospital— the Pethidine was enough to fog my brain. Now, as I fed my daughter, I noticed something wasn't quite right; she seemed like a floppy rag doll. Trying to make sense of this, I suddenly realised she was stoned.

"My God!" I yelled, "what am I doing? I have to stop tak ing drugs right now." It was a very painful decision. I wanted drugs, I felt I needed them to stop my internal pain. But my tiny, innocent daughter needed me more. That night I made a final decision to stop the madness. I felt pathetic. It had been a long time since I had recognised the real me. I knew that if I didn't stop taking pills, I would lose the only person I had ever truly loved, who was an indivisible part of me.

Next morning, when I told James about the Valium, he was angry with me. "Don't you see, Roxanne, when you take pills, Arizona receives the drug through your breast milk. Come on, give all the pills to me." I handed all my pills over to him, feeling vulnerable and naked. "Promise me you haven't hidden any, Rox," he said. I shook my head. I couldn't lie—if I did, I would be lying to my child.

I spent the rest of the day sitting in my room contemplating my fate. To me, having no pills was like having no air. As Arizona slept I sat watching the waves crashing on Palm Beach. I was alone, with only my thoughts to keep me company. When your life has been filled with turmoil and havoc, the normality of everyday living seems very strange. I really missed the madness, I found the silence deafening. A little flower caught my eye in the garden below, swaying to and fro in the breeze. It seemed a symbol of my unbalanced life.

In October 1995, my father and his wife Isabel flew out from Pfaltz in Germany to Australia. Psychologically I had waited for over twenty years to see him again. The moment he walked in the door, I felt a huge weight had lifted from my shoulders. At the same time I felt as though time had stood still. It was marvellous. My father looked older, but I felt as though I was five years old again. He gave me a huge hug and told me that he loved me, that he had always loved me. He admitted that he hadn't been a very good father, because of the divorce from my mother and the problems with their marriage, but he showed me that he wanted to try to make amends by telling me himself that he loved and cared for me. I am glad that he carne to see me, but a part of me feels as though there is now too much water under the bridge for us to have a real father and daughter relationship. I consider that James is my father, that my real father is simply a friend. But I am grateful that at least I now have some sort of relationship with my natural father. And, of course, I wasn't the perfect daughter, either. I finally forgave him for the pain and feeling of rejection he left me with. I am no longer a victim.

My mother and I now have a very good relationship. We have talked through our problems and I have forgiven her, as she has forgiven me, for the pain we caused each other. I love my mother dearly and always will. I realise now that my parents were definitely not suited to each other; my mother told me she only married my father to escape her own unhappy childhood— only to find that my father was abusive. My mother is a good woman at heart. I just think she lacked parenting skills. She herself was never loved as a child—and as a result she did not give love to her children. She was a victim of abuse and chose me as her emotional punching-bag. We were both victims, but the abuse and mistreatment will not be repeated with the next generation.

My mother and I talk regularly on the telephone, and for the past three years she has been able to tell me that she loves me. It is very hard for her to say those words, but I taught her by saying them myself every time I spoke to her. Now she feels comfortable about it. She has a very good relationship with her grandchildren, and is trying hard to make up for her bad parenting in the past. Like my father, she apologised for the hurt she had caused me. She told me that she had a bad temper and did not understand how rejected and battered she had made me feel. She came to Sydney for Christmas, 1995, and we talked about the past. Basically she told me she really loved all her children, but she didn't know how to be a good parent. Her marriage with my father was terrible—she used to feel there was no escape from it.

James, Jesse and I remain close. Without James I know that I would never have survived. I owe him my life. I have a dream that one day I will open a home for abused and unloved children. As my guardian angel told me, I still have things to do.

Being a mother has not been easy. I still battle agoraphobia, panic attacks and the remembered horror of my life. I visit a wonderful therapist, Dr Bennett. I have been drug free for over six years now, and I have become a writer. Every morning when I wake and see my daughter's beautiful face, it gives me the inspiration to free myself from the chains which have held me down for so long.

www.ingramcontent.com/pod-product-compliance
Lightning Source LLC
Chambersburg PA
CBHW031506270326
41930CB00006B/281